Granny D's
AMERICAN CENTURY

Also by

DORIS HADDOCK AND

DENNIS MICHAEL BURKE

GRANNY D

WALKING ACROSS AMERICA

IN MY 90TH YEAR

Granny D's
AMERICAN CENTURY

DORIS HADDOCK AND
DENNIS MICHAEL BURKE

University of New Hampshire Press
Durham, New Hampshire

UNIVERSITY OF NEW HAMPSHIRE PRESS
An imprint of University Press of New England
www.upne.com
© 2012 Dennis Michael Burke
All rights reserved
Manufactured in the United States of America
Designed by Eric M. Brooks
Typeset in New Caledonia, Smokler, and Vitrina
by Integrated Publishing Solutions

University Press of New England is a member of the
Green Press Initiative. The paper used in this book meets
their minimum requirement for recycled paper.

For permission to reproduce any of the material in this
book, contact Permissions, University Press of New England,
One Court Street, Suite 250, Lebanon NH 03766; or visit
www.upne.com

Library of Congress Cataloging-in-Publication Data
Haddock, Doris.
Granny D's American century / Doris "Granny D" Haddock
and Dennis Michael Burke.
    p. cm.
ISBN 978-1-61168-234-2 (cloth: alk. paper)—
ISBN 978-1-61168-235-9 (ebook)
1. Haddock, Doris. 2. Haddock, Doris—Childhood and
youth. 3. Haddock, Doris—Travel—United States.
4. Women political activists—United States—Biography.
5. Political activists—United States—Biography. 6. Older
women—United States—Biography. 7. New Hampshire—
Politics and government—1951– 8. Young women—
Massachusetts—Boston—Biography. 9. Depressions—
1929 Massachusetts—Boston. 10. Boston (Mass.)—
Biography. I. Burke, Dennis Michael. II. Title.
CT275.H235A3 2012   974.2'043092—dc23
    [B]   2011038793

5 4 3 2 1

To us survivors

CONTENTS

Preface ▪ ix
Introduction ▪ xi

BOOK I

1 Full Measure ▪ 3
2 Steaming into Life: 1928 ▪ 6
3 The Birthplace of Liberty, Including My Own ▪ 11
4 Castles and Princes ▪ 22
5 At Sea ▪ 31
6 Bubbles Burst ▪ 49
7 Jim's Girl ▪ 54
8 The Bohemians ▪ 61
9 Surviving by Our Wits ▪ 75
10 The Main Course of Life ▪ 87
11 Back to Harvard ▪ 98

BOOK II

12 On the Road Again ▪ 105
13 Alligators, Mermaids, Etcetera ▪ 109
14 Wake Up and Live ▪ 123
15 From the Very Balcony ▪ 140
16 Finding Life Everywhere ▪ 145
17 The Wind Shifts ▪ 153
18 Shared Courage ▪ 159
19 A Campaign from Our Town ▪ 164
20 Lessons from My Century ▪ 170

Last Delivered Speech ▪ 175
Last Undelivered Speech ▪ 177
Closing Note to the Reader ▪ 183

PREFACE

*W*e survivors of the Great Depression emerged from that time into a different world. Deep and long downturns like that one—and I suppose the present one—are occasions for new worlds to be born; the old ones never truly recover. That is mostly for the best, as these cycles are exactly the ambulation that moves us forward as individuals and as a civilization.

In the darkest days of the Depression we were told by President Franklin Delano Roosevelt—his full name was a calming mantra—that the only thing we had to fear was fear itself. That was wise counsel. Some of us did not heed the advice and later spent long years trying to escape fearful living and other people's shadows. It can be done, and at any age, but it is much easier getting into fear and shadows than out.

As for hard times generally, it is a fact that poor soils force the richest vintages. In these, my last days, I raise a toast to my Great Depression compatriots: we loved each other and worked and played very hard and with all the creativity we could muster. And I raise a toast to all of you who are doing your best during these present hard times.

This is a book about my days and nights as a young woman during the Depression, and my life as an old woman finally waking up to life again. My earlier memoir covers the other times of my life and my long walk. All these stories are offered as evidence that you can and must keep the spirit of adventure alive inside your heart long enough for it to someday reemerge. Life is a difficult choice between our loves and our fears. Love is the better use of a life, if you can find the courage for it. Love is hard, brave work, while fear is too easy—it is an early grave of comfy chairs and magazines and wasted heartbeats and hormones. In fact, I would rather you burned this book than used the reading of it as an excuse to not make some fresh trouble today.

For love and wisdom need representation in the world. The job is open and pays awfully well, if you care about the right things.

INTRODUCTION

*T*here is a glory of autumn leaves outside my big windows. I am an old woman among old trees in New Hampshire. You don't emotionally feel your true age, of course. You certainly feel it physically! But you are always something of a high schooler in your heart, and that is how it should be. That is the real you, and it is certainly the real me, but for the damned mirror.

Blue, a woman of twenty-five years, was earlier helping me dispose of my thousand books and other keepsakes as I prepared to move to the home of my son and daughter-in-law. The move would be but a short walk from my house through the woods to their home on the same creek. Blue was putting some things into my attic that I could not bear to give away. While she was doing that dusty work, I was, at the request of friends, finishing some words of advice regarding the sources of my strength over my many years—my hundredth birthday was less than a year away. Those words became this book now in your hands.

Blue showed me a little book from my library she thought curious—I was writing thank-you notes at my dining room table at the time. What should we do with this one? Give it away? Keep it? Toss it?

Blue is a rather tall sparkler of a young woman with vivid eyes, imaginative tattoos, and dark, curly hair. She was a compatriot from my latest adventure, camped now in a back bedroom until she could decide what to do next with her interesting life.

The book in her hand was *Expressive Voice Culture*, by Jessie Eldridge Southwick of Boston. I instantly pictured the author at the front of an Emerson College classroom in 1929: She stood perfectly erect and talked elegantly. She wrote beautiful script on the blackboard, holding the chalk in her white-gloved hands. The fingertips of her gloves were slightly floppy, and the explanation circulating among the students was that she had lost the tips of her fingers in a railway accident while accompanying her professor husband to a lecture engagement in New York City. She kept little corks inside her gloves to occupy the space of her missing fingertips. When I was a student, her book on elocution and expression was already a minor classic and would someday become translated worldwide.

I flipped through it now, with Blue standing near. You might think people would naturally know how to speak. They do not, especially according to this book. There are aspects to posture and things to know about the resonating chambers of the throat and sinus cavities that must be understood and subjected to rigorous practice. Every word must be given its due, and every syllable, too. We students recited the exercises at dawn and midday and dusk. I explained this to Blue.

I turned to the final page and read this aloud and in a proper Emersonian voice:

"Finally, by concentration of every distinctive phase, synthesized by a vital motive aroused by the message spoken, the voice becomes musical, forceful, clear, vibrant in the fulfillment of its natural function. The voice is the most potent influence of expression, the winged messenger between soul and soul."

I asked Blue to keep the book and to read it. Her own voice could be clearer, as might everyone's, and, indeed, she has a great deal to say, soul to soul, in this troubled world. We took a break for a macaroni lunch, which I prepared, and I thought I might tell her how I happened to have the book. It was from the days when Fear Itself stalked the world, and I was young.

Granny D's
AMERICAN CENTURY

Book 1

FULL MEASURE

I was born in 1910 on Walker Street in Laconia, New Hampshire. My father, a laborer, built the house, and we owned it free and clear. As a little girl I would recline in the summer lawn and pull little swords of grass apart to reveal their pale, sweet centers, which I would eat. Even now, I remember their smell and taste and cool touch upon the tongue. Good grass is quite healthy for you.

Laconia, then as now, stretches along snowmelt lakes that we skated in winter and boated in summer. The lakes were illuminated and made dreamy and musical on spring and summer evenings by stern-wheeled party boats from which laughter and clinking glasses and the music of foxtrot bands carried far across the water.

During World War I all that joy diminished; everything was dull and waiting, and the boat docks became slowly overgrown.

On a memorable summer afternoon of that time, an automobile approached beside the picket fence of our small home. I expect I sprang up from my cool recline in the grass. An automobile arriving was a great occasion, even if only a doctor on a house call—few others owned motorcars. An uncle stepped forth and commenced to talk Father into taking a war job in a Massachusetts shipyard. We soon moved away to a dreary place after selling our little house to a family who would accidentally burn it down.

Just after the armistice we moved back to Laconia and rented a place while we rebuilt on the old lot, which we bought back. We found ourselves standing one November 11th morning on the frosty chest of the town cemetery. We were there to honor the fresh graves of the war dead, whose spirits were still trudging back to town from Europe for burial. The old gentleman making the presentation to the gathered citizenry was reciting the Gettysburg Address from his weather-beaten memory. He struggled with ever more difficulty:

"It is rather for us to be here dedicated to the great task remaining before us, that from these honored dead we take increased . . . increased . . ."

"Devotion," the crowd whispered like a call-and-response prayer.

"Yes, devotion to that cause for which they, they gave the last fine, the last fine . . ."

"The last full measure," the reply came from us all.

"Yes, full measure of devotion."

At that point, he shrugged and smiled feebly; he couldn't remember another word. He had probably practiced for weeks and was too proud to carry a copy of the great speech, which would have been disrespectful to Lincoln, who was thought of in an almost religious aspect.

The Gettysburg Address, along with the Declaration of Independence, the Preamble to the Constitution, the names of the then forty-eight states, their capitals, the twenty-seven U.S. presidents (counting Grover Cleveland but once), were printed as back material in our tattered family dictionary. It was one of the two great books that enlightened our poor family, the other being, of course, the thesaurus.

I was but eight, but my mother knew I had recently been a visitor to those pages and had memorized long passages, including Lincoln's speech. She pushed me up onto the dais, and I stood beside the old man to take up his fallen torch. He took my hand as I spoke:

". . . that we here highly resolve that these dead shall not have died in vain; that this nation, under God, shall have a new birth of freedom, and that government of the people, by the people, for the people, shall not perish from the earth."

Many in the crowd could have recited it just as well, as the sea of moving lips testified. Their grandparents, after all, had known Lincoln and the Civil War. And all of us there-gathered had been down a long, hard road recently and lost more than a few neighbors and family. Shared suffering and imagination and emotional security are among the ingredients of empathy, and empathy is the rock of community. We truly mourned for each other's losses. My mother had lost her brother in the war and was especially low, though people tended to gather around such pain and soften it. She first knew he was dead when I thought I saw him in uniform in our house, but could not have.

She fainted into a chair when I told her what I had seen. In the greater stillness of those times, perhaps you could see subtler things.

As a town, we were taking a collective breath now. It is in such moments together — I had a white ribbon in my hair — when life seems, and most assuredly is, worth all the trouble. I wonder where that white ribbon might be now, nearly a century later. Is some piece of it now a bookmark in a forgotten attic? Are there at least a few threads of it holding tight to each other in deep forest soil somewhere?

What survived that day for me was the thrill of participation, of standing up. My young sights were suddenly set. I knew what I wanted to do.

*O*n a quiet Sunday, the platform of Laconia's modest railroad station was suddenly transformed by the steam braggadocio of an arriving southbound train. It rested impatiently to collect one passenger: me. I was eighteen. I hugged my parents, sisters, and brother. They were worried for me but confident of my moral toughness and therefore of my future; we were masters of our own destinies back then. My stout father, his bowler hat thumping in his fingers behind his back, made a quick inspection of the hunched locomotive. He was small against the high wall of black tubes and muscular steam torpedoes clustered beneath the engine's great riveted torso. Mushrooms of steam shot through the big-as-a-man iron-spoke wheels and across the iron knee bones connecting each wheel to the next. Father walked confidently through the coal-sweet steam, tipping his slight male salute — a nod hardly visible to females — to the engineer and the brakeman as he checked their eyes for reliability. Had he detected the red tint of rum or the glaze of exhaustion, I would have been on the next day's train instead. This great beast was to carry his little girl away to the city, and Father was powerless to do any more than to judge if its struts and tubes and men seemed up to the high responsibility. These trains were perhaps the first big bit of technology to stand against our sense of having control over the things around us — things that increasingly held mortal sway over our families and futures. But Father was not cowed.

Why is that cylinder there dripping oil?" he asked of the brakeman.

"Because I just oiled it, bud," came the curt reply. Father didn't mind the tone; it was business, and he was satisfied.

After all that, and after a third or fourth chorus of Mother reminding me of the proper conduct of young girls in big cities, I felt myself boosted up by Father's stevedore arms to the balancing reach of a bearded conductor. In the transfer, Father's hat went rolling along the platform, and Rex, my fourteen-year-old brother, fetched it and put it on his own small head. They all waved: Rex waved from under the hat. My three sisters waved sadly; Mother and Father waved bravely.

Just inside the vestibule and holding tight to my carpetbag, I blew kisses and got teary-eyed and began my journey away from home on the very Boston & Maine train that had whistled through the air of all my growing up. It had taken my brightest high school chums, one by one, away to college and to glory the year before. What dreams lay off across the air split by this whistle? I had wished the wish that now was my reality, if I dared pinch myself.

The Boston & Maine was building speed now out of the station and blasting its whistle across the town and across the lake for anyone to hear: Extry! Extry! Dottie Rollins is finally getting the hell out of Tiny Town!

Laconia slid by the windows like a diorama; every important place — especially the pink granite library that had been my castle — now seemed trivial. Even the furniture warehouse where my father was the sole employee looked like any other hulking building. My father single-handedly pulled impossible loads of furniture up the building's high elevators by means of ropes and pulleys. A great bear he was — a bear with tools who built our little house twice himself and bellowed to keep his five children, mostly me, in line. He complained about the world as he read the morning newspaper. He was a Lincoln Republican — all for self-sufficiency in himself and others, but intensely moderate in accommodating the opinions and needs of others. There is hardly such a thing today. He had given me a fistful of pencils and a stack of paper and envelopes that I might write home every evening, which I would do for a long time — postage was two cents and delivery was twice a day, to homes, and four times a day to businesses. You might receive the reply to your morning dinner invitation by afternoon.

The train slid past the last little houses. Every dark space in the landscape turned the window into a mirror, and I saw myself: bobbed brown hair, roundy face, oversized brown eyes, undersized bosom.

I traveled that day almost alone; a newspaper-engrossed gentleman sitting grandly among the sinews of his own cigar smoke was the only fellow passenger within view. The railway car had little dining tables, but there would be no food service that Sunday. If one were desperate for the full experience, one could stumble forward to the half-asleep attendant in the dining car for a cup of coffee. I did so and returned to my little table with it steaming and awful — I had wasted the first nickel of my adult life.

We raced our coal-fired shadow across crystalline snowdrifts, sending up diamonds that melted on the window beside my eye as I rested my head in a tiny draft of fresh air. *The quality of mercy is not strain'd. It droppeth as the gentle rain from heaven.* Any drop of rain, any melted snowflake often brought those lines to my mind. The lines of Portia in *The Merchant of Venice* had been so drilled into me by my high school English teacher, Grammy Swain, that they were sometimes like a song I could not get out of my head.

In the curves, the long engine revealed itself, straining ahead, its parts pumping furiously. The landscape beyond was overexposed and as elegantly arranged as if by the Japanese — the least possible lines indicating farms, fences, forests, outcroppings of gray granite in the snow. Inside, the presto metronome of the rails and the Empire perfume of coal and cigar and old upholstery blended with the morning honey — a smoky nebula pierced by the ornate gleamings of this well-worn rocket ship's polished brass and cut glass.

Maybe the man deep in his newspaper owned this train and I was his new young consort who would make him do good deeds in the world. Maybe I was his long-lost daughter and would momentarily reveal my identity to him. Maybe I owned this railroad and the gentleman was my difficult but lovable banker, who was slowly dying from having been chlorine gassed in the war, but who would not give up his cigars or his loyal affection for me.

I should have liked a young seatmate to share the beauty and my mixed feelings — mostly my excitement. I sat near the center of the long car, hoping some handsome vagabond yet loose in the train would come sit by me. But it was Sunday, and respectable people and interesting people — I was hoping for the latter — were elsewhere. I thought it odd and a little rude for the gentleman to be smoking a billowing cigar, but then I noticed ashtrays everywhere and realized I had taken a seat in the smoking car. Not wishing to look any more stupid than necessary, I fished a stylish Murad cigarette from my bag and added to the blue haze of our rocket salon.

Closer to Boston, the man with the cigar came over and stood around me, refolding his newspapers and lurching gently within his smoke coils. He commenced some small talk, congratulating me for going off to college, "if all that works out for you." He had that gentle disdain—you could see he was trying to be modern and overcome it—for women who did not stay and cook and have babies. He suggested that I was brave to be heading into this economy. I could not imagine what he was talking about, as the economy was booming, and had been so for seven or eight years.

He may have just then been reading some negative newspaper story. Indeed, it was true that 1 percent of Americans owned 40 percent of the nation's wealth, and the new rich were using their political muscle to have their income taxes knocked down more each year. It was true that the middle class was less than a fifth of the nation; most American families earned less than $750 a year—only $275 for farm families. It was true that automatic machines were eliminating hundreds of thousands of good jobs each year. It was true that labor unions had fallen to a fraction of their membership of ten years previous. It was true that huge corporations were buying up family-based, town-based industries and shutting them down to make monopolies; two hundred corporations now controlled half the industrial economy. Hardworking Americans had become nearly twice as productive as a decade earlier, but the extra profits were not going to them.

Maybe the fellow thought it was all heading for a fall. Maybe he saw how housing construction and automobile sales were falling off, and how American farmers were going bust by the bushel basket. Maybe the decline in furniture shipments that my father noticed in the warehouse would have figured into this man's mood had he known. But if he was indeed gloomy in his outlook—and his cigar tip glowed red like a warning lamp every time he paused between ominous comments—he was certainly not representing the common view. Times were good and getting better, is what most of us thought. If you had some money in the stock market, you saw it grow by 30 or 40 percent that year.

People were mortgaging their homes to get in on the stock market, as the sky was the limit. Victorious America was taking over the world, after all.

Rain began pouring down the windows.

"Did you bring an umbrella?" he asked me.

"Of course," I lied for some silly reason. You should never lie about umbrellas; your punishment will come swiftly.

The Birthplace of Liberty, Including My Own

3

*I*t was still pouring when I arrived at Boston's North Station: 3:31 p.m. Sunday, January 6, 1929. This exactitude derives from old train schedules and not memory, though I do remember the journey clearly and can yet smell the cigar smoke in my hair.

The sidewalks by the station were black-scaled with pumping wet umbrellas; the streets were a-splash with clattering Model T Fords liberally honking their oogah-oogah horns—which were a Laurel-and-Hardy comedy effect even then. There were also many of the new Fords—the Model As—and of course a mix of more exotic, sometimes even colorfully appointed cars known to me from their glamorous magazine ads: the Essex, Whippet, Studebaker, Auburn, Franklin, Plymouth, Pontiac, Hudson, Nash, Chevrolet, Cadillac, Hupmobile, Chrysler, Dodge Brothers, Buick, Oldsmobile, DeSoto, Packard. I was amazed by the utter wealth splashing by me every second. I saw what I thought must be a Duesenberg—so incredibly long and fancy—from which we took the term "a real duesy."

I couldn't imagine what so many people were doing humping along on a Sunday, a day quite dead back home in Laconia. These people seemed grimly focused on their processions. They had jobs, I suppose, as the stock market crash—the opening act of the Great Depression—was nearly a year off. I decided not to be frightened by the utter chaos of the city before me. I looked upon the scene instead as an elaborately choreographed stage waiting just for me—its actors already in motion and expecting my entrance. The rain was for dramatic effect.

I was free and eighteen—nearly nineteen.

I had just escaped from the Scott & Williams silk stocking loom factory in Laconia, where I worked for a monotonous year and a half after high school. I got that job easily because I was a minor star in the well-attended plays produced by the high school and the community playhouse. In those days, the available town entertainment was entirely of that sort, plus motion pictures.

The plant manager at Scott & Williams, a slightly hunched Mr. Woolridge — whose handsome son, a violin-playing poet I worshipped from afar — brought the weekly pay envelopes personally to each of the several hundred of us and always handed mine to me with a Shakespearean flourish. I never knew if he was genuinely impressed with my acting or if he was mocking my descent from local star to slave-wage factory girl. He probably did not know himself — just something amusing to stitch into the drab fabric of his week.

That was all history. I was now in the big city of Boston, presenting as cutely as I could manage.

My part in this day's drama was to be comic. The rain increased; it would rain nearly an inch and a half in a short time, bringing unseasonable warmth to the city. Stepping in and out of the station, looking for my host, I was soon drenched. Black dye was streaming down my face from the little cloche hat my mother had bought for me. The long feather that had curled elegantly downward, Clara Bow style, from the top of the hat to just under my chin was now sagging like the dead bird it was. The black fur collar of my new long woolen coat, purchased from the same sharp gentleman in Laconia (who had winked at me even as he hoodwinked my mother) was revealed by the drench to be hardly the rain-resistant rabbit fur as advertised, but the cheap fur of a smelly skunk. In the store, I had stood before a full-length mirror and seen myself for the first time as a grown woman, something of a flapper, a femme fatale.

"A little doll!" the shopkeeper said.

"Not bad," my mother agreed. She had grown up just when motion pictures — silent ones — were coming onto the scene, and she had wished stardom of some sort for herself. She had absolutely no opportunity in that regard, but she could now pack her genes off in the person of me, and I was happy to oblige her dreams. I had my sights set on the New York stage, however, not "whorehouse Hollywood."

In any case, my mother was pleased to have a little doll to send forth, and I did look pretty good for at least the first half-minute or so in the Boston rain.

The black dye of the cloche was now hemorrhaging down my face — I could see it reflected in the windows of the station's great doors. Well, I assured myself, I know how to play comedy. I stepped fully outside again to find my mark where I was to be met. The rain doubled, blurring the street scene.

"Dottie! Over here!" a skinny college boy was shouting and waving from across the way, urging me to hazard the street and save him the trouble. I splashed across the roaring jungle stream. I did not recognize the fellow at first; he was certainly not the meaty young fellow I was expecting.

I thought I was waiting for Alan Ayer, a boy from school who had moved to Boston right after our graduation. He had made all the arrangements for my lodging and my first job, and said he would meet me at the station and take me to a rooming house in Somerville, just north of Cambridge. At the last minute, however, he was not able to come for me. His best friend from high school, Bob Dinsmore, who was tall and thin, fast walking and stern, appeared instead, just late enough for me to be so drenched.

"Alan has a date," he yelled over the million blunt bullets of rain hitting sooted awnings. "One of his big blondes—you know how it is." We were running. I rather did know that Alan preferred big blondes. I was a brunette, naturally, and not big in any department. Little Dottie was my usual nickname, which fit me all over.

Bob Dinsmore was from a wealthy family, and I was not. This favor he was doing for Alan was a bit like fetching a new maid from the station on a day when you had meant to be playing tennis with someone named Alice, except for the rain. Bob's twin sister was actually a friend of mine. The Dinsmores, being among the town's elite, did not allow their children to attend the public dances in our town. She and I were friends just the same, and she envied me for getting to go to the big town affairs.

None of this history seemed to be helping me with Bob, who had brusquely grabbed one handle and half the weight of my big carpetbag. He was being quite unfriendly, literally pulling me along and shouting for me to keep up as he bumpered us through the flooded city. We jumped on a bus, then an elevated train, then a subway, then another bus. He rushed us through an impossible urban maze; I realized I could never find my way back alone. There were stores and theaters and large homes and apartments everywhere. Winter snowbanks along the sidewalks were melting in the warm rain, revealing from their glaciers long-lost gloves and oddities.

We passed by famed Harvard Yard, thick with fine-looking young men, even on a Sunday, dashing most dashingly through the rain. Just seeing them and their buildings was magical to me. The marquee of a half-demolished motion picture theater was still advertising its final show: *The Last Command*. It was not a talkie, but no doubt there had been an organist up front. Talkies were still quite amazing to us. Al Jolson's *The Jazz Singer* had come out only a year or so earlier.

I had seen *The Last Command* back home a year earlier. It was a movie within a movie: the story of an officer from the Russian czar's army who, after the Revolution, ended up as a minor actor in Hollywood. Playing the part of a commander in battle, he gave, quite outside the script, so rousing a speech to his soldiers that it was clear he had mentally reverted to old times and real wars. He then majestically died and was pronounced a great man by the actor playing the director. It was a fine film—Josef von Sternberg, Emil Jannings, and William Powell. Seeing it in such dilapidated circumstances was like seeing a respected townsman in a dream, out of place on skid row. It worried me; I would rather have seen a black cat crossing our path.

We finally walked along a sidewalk between Cambridge and Somerville. The rain had let up, but the walk was endless. The sidewalk extended so far ahead that I thought I could see the curvature of the earth. Bob is going to walk me all the way back to New Hampshire, is what I thought. The other thing I thought was that I was going to need a boyfriend with an automobile. My every stitch and feather was sagging and dripping and I just couldn't imagine why the Dinsmores had sent Bob off to school without a car. If Bob cared to be in the running for me, he was out, as far as I was concerned.

In addition to our class difference, it seems I had more positively offended Bob the year previous. My offense had to do with the fact that I, so theatrical and funny, had been chosen to divine the futures of my classmates at a pregraduation assembly. I lost several friends in the process. I tried to remember the prophecy that had so offended him.

I believe I predicted an engagement to some girl he loathed but his family loved. Alan Ayer had suggested I do it as a prank, assuring me it would be funny. It wasn't to Bob, or probably to the girl.

The four-story white rooming house in Somerville, finally in view, was nicely framed by crystalline trees and the white forms of shrubs beneath the snow. A satisfied-looking Alan Ayer was waiting on the wide porch for me, having completed his other duties and now come to apologize and see that I was properly introduced to Mrs. Parker, the landlady. The rain stopped, and the sun came out long enough to sparkle for an instant in the glazed snowbank beside the front walk. Alan stood there atop the steps like the owner, like the mayor, though he was only a few months older than me and nearly as poor. He looked at my stained and bedraggled self, laughed, and said, "Dottie, old girl, you look like you need a little drinkie."

He met up with us again in the parlor with some alcoholic concoctions to "warm us up." Indeed. I had already concluded that he was, in this new setting, an expert at warming up the girls, and I took but a sip of the poison. I had promised my parents I would not drink alcohol in Boston. Prohibition was full on, and rumors were rampant of people going blind from drinking poorly made bathtub gin.

Mrs. Parker, a laughing redhead in her forties, with a thick Boston accent and a bean-fed body with a grand front, greeted me with open arms. "Our little movie stah," she said, pulling me suddenly into her pulchritude—I recognized "My Sin," the latest perfume to flood the market and evidently her front range. I smiled but was secretly offended. Actress, yes. Big star, inevitably—but movies? No. I was intent upon the stage, not Hollywood. I read the celebrity news stories like every other girl and understood exactly how it happened that bad girls got good film parts. I think I made an exception for Clara Bow, a star who looked rather like me, I fancied, and was my size. Just the same, I would stick to Broadway, where it was on the up-and-up, or so I believed. After the conversation had half moved on to the next subject, I belatedly blurted that movies would not be to my liking. I was defending my honor in these new quarters.

In that moment I had resolved to be my own person in this new world, even if my mother was more than willing to look the other way for me to be a movie star. Mother was a practical woman.

The only bright light that could fall on a woman in those days seemed to be sunlight in the farm fields or the klieg above actors, so I do not fault myself for yearning for the stage. I don't mean to suggest that I was just looking for the spotlight in life, but you do want your life to be something worth the effort and pain. You want to make a difference somehow, and you want that difference to be noticed and appreciated—you can't help wanting that. There weren't many ways for women to get all that.

Alan tried to get me to down my drinkie. I declined.

Despite his having sent a rude agent to deliver me from the train station, and despite his overexuberance now as a host, I held him in the highest esteem. Only a few weeks earlier I had been at a Christmas dance in Laconia when he changed my world. He was the one person from Laconia High whom everyone knew and liked. At the holiday dance, he, our former class president, made a triumphant return from his new life in Boston, where he worked at Harvard by day and studied law at Suffolk in the evenings—you could go directly from high school to law school back then, perhaps because life was shorter and there was little time to waste.

I sat with the girls and watched him pump his handshake among the other boys. Quite a Jay Gatsby he was (we were all reading that book)—marvelous looking and suave beyond his years.

The girls sat over here and the boys over there. Brave boys would come the long way across the dance floor to ask a girl to dance. It would be a long walk back for him if she declined. Girls would keep their dance cards in their heads: "Yes, I would be delighted. There are four boys ahead of you. You will be right after Roger." You might have to keep a dozen or more names correctly in your head. The boys would have to remember their place or forever be thought cads for not showing up in time. A local foxtrot band would provide the music. The Charleston would be danced several times through the evening. Since Lindbergh's big hop over the Atlantic the year of our graduation, a Charleston variation called the Lindy Hop was the biggest thing of all.

Tall, dark Alan walked across the big floor, lighting it up as he came, and I knew he would not be turned away by any of the girls.

Remarkably, he walked up to *me*.

He asked me to dance.

I was completely available, having arrived only a short time earlier and not being too much of an attraction anyway. I was small and funny and well regarded by the boys as a confidante, but they did not take me seriously as a girlfriend.

I had changed, though, and Alan noticed before the others—perhaps because he had been away and also because he cared to notice people. I'm quite sure that he cared about people in the same professional way that an art curator cares for his collection. Alan would be the first to notice any cracks in your varnish and give you some constructive advice for it, but always on the purely positive side. He would also be the first to notice your young body changing. He would not be too shy to look at you up and down and smile. Had he asked to see it sans drapery, one might have thought about it, for his concerns seemed somehow elevated, nearly clinical. But of course he was a gentleman and did not ask such a thing. As gentlemen can be such bores.

Mercifully, ours was neither foxtrot nor Charleston but a slow dance, so we were close and we talked. He told me that I had become quite better looking, a compliment of sorts. He asked why I was still in Laconia.

"Here you are, Doris, more than a year and a half since we graduated, and you're not on Broadway. What gives? You can't enjoy working at that damned factory—that's not for you."

He even correctly had me on Broadway, not in Hollywood. He was attentive to detail that way—a marvelous listener who cared to remember what you said.

I explained that I still had my big dreams, but the cost of Emerson College of Oratory in Boston, the only serious acting and liberal arts college within imaginable geographic range, was simply out of reach for now. I told him that I was saving up, which was true.

"Nonsense," he replied, leading us through a lovely turn. "Life is short. You can do just what I do: work at Harvard by day and go to your own college at night. Emerson is not too far from Harvard. I'll set it up for you. You'll have to get admitted to Emerson by yourself, of course, but I can easily get you a job at the Harvard Business School, which—I suppose because it is more for the class of boys who will have to work at jobs in their lives—is on the other side of the river from the main campus, which puts it closer to Emerson. And I know a good place where you can stay. Just give the factory your two weeks' notice tomorrow, and I'll do the rest. I'll send you the details in a few days."

You might not believe that people were like that, but they were: full of confidence for themselves and for you, and ready to take definitive action right now. It was the kind of confidence that had built the British Empire, and now it was our way of thinking, too.

He said it as if we were arranging a picnic. All I could do was marvel and continue dancing with a big smile. Life is so easy, Doris. A state of mind, Doris. A bloody picnic. Sometimes the drawbridge of the grail castle just opens, and in you go, dancing—and you had damned well better take the opportunity when it comes, as the big door closes as quickly as it opens.

"It's a very kind offer," I said to him. "I'll see what my father says."

I hesitated a whole day to tell my family. I hesitated because I sensed my life about to change. I was savoring it. I watched the sun of my girlhood go down one more time.

How cold New Hampshire suddenly seemed! Boston was only a little ways south, but it was south enough to be Rio de Janeiro in my mind, full of bright sun and carnivals.

Mother and Father thought it was a grand idea. Alan had suggested it, after all, and he was trusted and admired even by the adults of the town. My sisters helped me pack my few things right after the holiday. I had but one good outfit to see me through my first year, though I would change it with a hundred borrowed capes and scarves and belts.

Landlady Parker, who seemed to know my whole story and whom Alan had telephoned the day after the dance to reserve a spot for me, was blotting a tea towel on my streaked face, as Mr. Dinsmore had not even offered his handkerchief during our trip across town.

"Let's go into the bathroom, dear," she said. It was something of a surprise: I was fairly new to fully indoor bathrooms in the first place, and the idea of ladies going in together was altogether novel. She scrubbed my face in earnest and straightened my hat's long feather as best she could, understanding that the feather was part of the look and had to stay.

The boys soon took their leave, with Alan promising to walk me to my new job the next morning. He winked at Mrs. Parker as he left.

"You will have your very own room as soon as I can manage," she said to me as she watched the departing boys through the Irish lace of the door window. This comment upset my expectations.

"Until then, you're going to share a room with little Gladys, who is very sad. I know you can comfort her." She was now patting dry the fragrant collar of my coat, hanging near the front door. "This is a little gamy, isn't it, dear?" she said.

"Let me tell you about Gladys. Her heart was recently broken, and she needs a sensitive friend. Just keep reminding her—will you?—that there are plenty of fish in the sea. She needs to understand that. Lots and lots and lots of handsome fishes." She said it as she patted and smoothed the fur.

She then rested her long hand on my shoulder and gave me a dying mother look. "You will be that friend for her, won't you, Doris?" I nodded and smiled.

"Is she pretty?" I inquired. It was not a strange thing to ask back then.

"Oh, very," she replied.

Gladys, she told me, had followed her high school sweetheart to Harvard from somewhere in the Carolinas. At his encouragement, she left her job in a textile mill. He ditched her as soon as he met a cute college girl. There were no girls admitted to Harvard, of course, but Harvard's sister school was Radcliffe, located right next door—not simply as a biological convenience, but that, too.

I asked Mrs. Parker if Alan seemed to have a girlfriend. It was an innocent question, and I was merely curious—it's a natural thing to wonder about. She informed me that another girl in this same house, presently out of town, seemed to be attached to him, and he to her. But she didn't know how seriously. She looked a little upset.

"He seems to be piling them up pretty high," she said as she took the glasses into the kitchen.

I settled upstairs, waiting for Gladys to return from an evening church service. There were not two beds, but one, almost a cot, cheaply made but wide. It had a flat, squeaky grid of metal straps and springs under a thin mattress. It would have made a better trampoline than bed.

I found room in the closet for my few things, and then explored the hall to find the upstairs washroom. I flushed the toilet several times to make sure I had the thing mastered. Like most toilets of that day, it had a water tank near the ceiling that made a great noise when it sent the water down. I then looked out my window at the slushy street until I got bored of it growing dark. I tried to read a magazine. Finally, I turned off all but a dim nightlight and went to bed.

Some time later I heard little Gladys come up the stairs and approach along the wooden hallway. The creaking of the old floor suggested the movement of consequential mass.

The door squeaked open. I instantly imagined Queequeg the harpooner, come to share a bed with Ishmael. Like Ishmael, I feigned sleep and peeked at the stranger undressing. She was pretty of face in the dim light. The poor girl was indeed a bit large, and I easily calculated her handicap in her sad competition with some svelte Radcliffe girl.

She was soon in her shortie nightgown, a ruffled piñata of considerable yardage. Without warning, the brave little forklift of her legs dropped her bale of rump hard onto the bed. I was ejected upward and could no longer play the scene dead. Seeing my contorted face in the air, she squealed.

We introduced ourselves, and she remembered that I was expected. She had forgotten. She had stayed at church to talk to a minister and had lost track of the details of the day. I consoled her for her loss — though never having had a steady boyfriend myself, it was mostly acting as I stretched my empathy to a new place. I was truly thinking: My goodness, what's the unholy fuss? There are so many boys in the world, and all similarly equipped and similarly motivated. I may have mentally excluded Alan, as he was a little special — and richer boys generally.

She wriggled into a huge fetus, coiling tight, then uncoiling, puffing a pillow, facing around toward me, then away. I gripped the metal frame under the edge of the mattress to anchor myself against these waves. She turned and turned, and I began to feel queasy as the room spun. She then began to quietly sob, apologizing for it. Each sob effected a bounce of this little raft upon the sea. I just "went with it," as they say: I imagined our boat to be the yacht of a great Broadway star — my yacht — moored on the starboard side of Manhattan. Then finally, nearly ill, I decided to not think of boats at all. I decided the only thing to do was to try to think of something sad so that I might take some of her burden.

I pulled up a memory I had always used to help me tear-up when I needed to weep in an acting scene: A boy named Tommy, in my grade school class, was very poor and dressed in very handed-down clothes, yet he had great dignity. One of our teachers said something to him that riled him up; I don't know what it was, but it may have been about his appearance or about his family circumstance. He talked sharply in return. So she had him stand there straight while she slid a yardstick behind his belt, a little ways into the small of his back, then took wide adhesive tape and taped across his eyes, then to the back of his head where the stick was. Then she taped his mouth closed and taped around again to the back, then a few more times around him, so that he looked to all the world like a martyr at the stake to be burned. She then led him roughly by an ear from class to class, saying, "This is what happens to naughty boys." He stood as tall and proud as a four-star general, with his chin out and his shoulders square. I thought, how brave and dignified! I cried terribly for him, putting my head down on my desk and sobbing. Others were staring at him wide-eyed or laughing. I could not help but bawl for him. He had a shock of brown hair mussed by the tape. She would yank at the tape to hurt his skin or pull his hair. "This, this is what happens to naughty boys, and this." With every "this" she would yank the tape to hurt him again, but he would not flinch or give her any satisfaction.

This abuse of power, the sight of which I believe slightly changed the direction of my life—a change of perhaps only one degree that would nevertheless sail me into new seas over time—so enraged me that I felt like knocking her down, but I did not have the courage or strength. So I cried.

Remembering it in bed, and listening to Gladys sob and sob after the cruelty of her boyfriend's disloyalty, I got into the spirit and cried with her. The nausea went away as we bounced along. Then she settled down, and we embraced—as girls often did back then without it meaning anything—and we cried each other finally to sleep. I was sorry for Gladys and her no-good boyfriend and her ruined life. It moves me even now.

4

CASTLES AND PRINCES

*A*lan took me to Harvard the next morning as promised. The city was brightly enameled by the rain and was heavily scented by breakfasts wafting from cracked-open windows. People on the sidewalk seemed manifestly unfriendly, however, as if they had just read a very unfair newspaper article about us. I would smile at them to no effect. Alan, I noticed, did not smile or even slightly tip his hat, as he certainly would have done back home. That coldness was but small change, and the walk was otherwise marvelous, for all the unfriendly people had somehow managed to build a beautiful city. The smell of wet soil, wet bricks, automobile fumes, the rumble and hum of the sprawling, soaring city, the presence somewhere of Emerson College of Oratory all pulled me along like smoke through some new-to-me erotic urban sensibility. I was on Alan's diamond leash, nearly skipping beside him. The dreamy scenery of Harvard Yard's old buildings then folded around us—castles grander than the Laconia Library and so many of them, all arranged nicely—with young men striding down straight shortcuts to family-arranged destinations. One might ride piggyback on any of them into a beautiful life.

"That building there, the Wadsworth House, the yellow one, was where General George Washington set up his first headquarters in the first battles of the Revolution," Alan said. "The house was already fifty years old at the time. And Emerson later lived there as a student."

I couldn't believe it. Its eaves were modestly dripping yesterday's rain like any other building.

"And Longfellow's old house is just up Brattle Street there, which was also Washington's headquarters after this place, and up that same street is the yard of the blacksmith shop where the spreading chestnut tree stood—I'll show you on the way back this evening. They cut down the tree about fifty years ago to widen the street, but the schoolchildren had a chair made of the wood and gave it to old Longfellow when he was about dead, and you can go into the house, which is a museum now, and sit in that chair when Longfellow's grandson, who runs the place, isn't looking." It was as if he was pulling my leg, but I knew he wasn't, as he didn't joke at all. I had fallen Alice-like into a history book.

We walked through the main streets of Cambridge, then across the bridge over the Charles River to the Harvard Business School, where we entered the great dining hall—it may as well have been a cathedral, so grand. The experience was religious, sacramental—I expect I bowed my head a little going in. Had he been taking me to the kitchen to be carved up for the gentlemen's lunch and noon sacrifice, I think I would have gone.

Alan introduced me to my new boss, a pretty, dark-haired young woman named Alice who seemed to take Alan's every suggestion as some newly enacted law to be carefully understood and followed. I marveled at his power over women—my landlady and now this Alice. I had loved walking down the sidewalk with him, listening to his historic tour along the way and his little mentions of his law school. But he was best observed when telling ladies what to do, just as he had told me what to do with my life on that dance floor.

It would be nice to think I was that iconic American free woman, new to a job in the city, her beret tossed high in the air, her attitude feisty for equality—but that describes a woman who hardly yet existed, except in the matter of voting. That is how very long ago this was—though an instant ago to me. For us, at the end of the Roaring Twenties, young women were infantilized, and boyfriends were called daddies, and we pretty much thought it was the cat's meow.

My job would be to set the tables for several hundred students, all men; I was to check their meal cards as they arrived. Alan told me, somewhat aside, that there would be a good deal of switching around of these cards by the students, allowing some boys who might have otherwise missed a meal to get fed, and I should look the other way so nobody went hungry. "There's plenty of food, after all," Alan told me. "Harvard is richer than John D. Rockefeller."

So I was now a checker girl and a table setter, and I got right to it. Even that first day, the Harvard boys seemed to enjoy talking with me. Maybe it was because I was new or maybe because I was small-town friendly, or maybe because I was confident in conversation. Maybe it was because the few clothes I brought were stylish enough to pass for a society girl.

The first days flew. Several young men were soon giving me books to read—things they were particularly excited to share. The current big read was Oswald Spengler's *Decline of the West*. As the Harvard boys were generally darlings, I agreed to read many of the same books over and over and was, after several readings of the same books, thought to be a quick study. Spengler came in two volumes, the second of which was quite new at the time. Spengler's point was that we of Western civilization were admirable dreamers whose fates were nevertheless nearing an end point; our wild ride, our successes, our wealth, our democratic freedoms, were all on a runaway trolley about to come off the rails. Reading Spengler was perhaps preparing us to accept the coming dark clouds. He was also freeing the more daring artists to break away from old patterns and create very new styles. I doubt that the modernism of poetry, novels, painting, or architecture would have been quite the same without him. He helped fulfill his own prophecies, as his books certainly helped pave the way for the idea that democracies and republics were on the way out, and that strong men, including FDR, who was still unknown to most of us, and the dark-side leaders of Europe—already on the scene—were somehow inevitable. There were all kinds of gangsters around, really—the strongman archetype was clearly ascendant. In February, the St. Valentine's Day Massacre happened in Chicago. It was disgusting, but not so much that we stopped spending our dimes on gangster movies. Power and force were very in, and the value of human life, thanks to industrialization and World War I, was a penny stock falling fast.

For now, there were still great social traditions of respect and kindness. Alan, who had moved up the Harvard kitchen ranks, was gentleman enough to visit me nearly every day to see how I was doing. From time to time he said something to remind me of my dream—my reason for coming to town. He wasn't exactly nagging me about going into downtown Boston to apply at Emerson, but he didn't want me to forget my dream.

I began going out with a Harvard boy, just to the movies and for ice cream; my life as a checker girl soon seemed rather perfect. I kept finding things to do rather than go apply at Emerson. What if they turned me down? How would I explain that to my friends and family? It was somehow easier not to go. Months went by and spring was finally in the air. Cambridge and Somerville were fragrant with garden mulch and blossoms.

As I started to have a little spare money, I bought a few magazines about entertainment figures. When I was younger, I, like most girls, kept a scrapbook of photos and news stories about singers and actors and actresses. We would cut them from our parents' discarded magazines such as the *Saturday Evening Post, Collier's, Woman's Home Companion*, and several others. I prided myself on cutting the clippings very neatly and arranging them artfully in my book. I think I had the finest star scrapbook in my high school. We made our own glue from flour and water. The scrapbooks were opened and shared to make easy conversation, just as young people today visit on their computers, sharing little things they find in the news.

But by the late '20s there were actual star magazines, and now I had the money for them. But the pictures of the stars made me think sadly of my mother back home. She had sent me off to become a big something and save her from her life of monotony and deprivation. Was it not my own dream as well? I think it was. And I might have kept drifting away from that dream if not for Alan.

"I have made a map to help you get to Emerson," he said one day in March. His map included bus numbers, travel times, and every turn of sidewalk.

Alan was not giving me special attention; he gave this sort of service to all his friends and was rather famous for it. He was so well regarded back home, as I mentioned, that my father did not hesitate in granting permission for my move to Boston. "If Alan Ayer is making the arrangements," he said, "that is good enough. I would trust him with our lives." So Alan was now my guardian angel, refusing to let me get off the track of my dreams for another season. Maybe he felt responsible for getting me to the city and would not want to be criticized for it going sour.

Alan was a fine-looking young man, tall, dark-haired, dark-eyed, with broad shoulders and the look of a future corporate kingpin or senator. It was fun to walk mornings beside him from Somerville to Harvard, as I often did, and sometimes also with his girlfriends, who were nice enough. I could not help but be attracted to Alan, though I was sure his interest in me was purely friendship and town loyalty, nothing more. I tried not to think of it otherwise. Just the same, throughout your life you will come upon just a very few people who constantly care and consciously remind you who you are and what you might yet do in the world. Alan was such a person for me, and I rather loved him for it.

His map was perfect. It had to be if I were to get back in time for the evening dining service. The near impossibility of that challenge had discouraged me from even trying, so Alan's exact instructions and minute-to-minute bus schedule gave me the push to finally do it.

I followed his instructions like a worried spy and was finally in front of 30 Huntington in Copley Square, looking up at the windows of Emerson. I went up the stairs and asked to speak with someone in admissions. The office receptionist, a student, called someone to see if I could be seen. The student seemed just a few years older than I was. She smiled and said, "Right this way, Miss Rollins." She said it so funny, as though we were old friends playing office; her hand was on my shoulder as we sped down the hall. She told me her name was Lulu and that she thought my outfit was cute and she hoped I got accepted because Emerson was heavenly fun. She escorted me into a modest office where a grim, older woman sat behind a grand desk. She rose and shook my hand, then we both sat and I made my pitch. I ran through my acting credits, and I described my Broadway dreams and my need to work days and my situation at Harvard, which I thought might be just a little impressive.

"Well, Doris," she finally said, smiling with the stiffened lips of hard news, "as it happens we do not have night classes."

The whole theory of my new life fell apart in that instant. Alan had not done this particular bit of homework for me, or maybe he had, but trusted that I could find my way around it. Dreams are worth their uncertainties, and we cannot demand that every risk ahead be identified and resolved before we begin, or it would hardly be an adventure.

I was well dressed for the meeting. I held my poise in the face of this bad news. I let some silence into the room, which is always a good idea when you want the other person to take a step in your direction. Indeed, the woman seemed to see something in me.

"As you have come all this way, perhaps we can ask you to read a few lines in our auditorium."

She went to a file cabinet and pulled out a scene for me to memorize.

"Follow me," she said.

Walking through the halls with her, seeing how she was bowed to by staff and students, made me understand she was the director of the school or someone even grander. She put me in a little room where I was to have fifteen minutes alone with the lines, which she handed me.

"See if you can memorize a good part of this," she said as she left. I opened the folder. It was Portia from *The Merchant of Venice*.

"I'll do my best," I called after her. These were the lines Grammy Swain had beaten into me in high school.

The trick with an oft-heard speech like Portia's is to make it come alive with human personality. I would try to make it new and my own—to make the words seem as though I had just thought them up.

She and one other person, a man, were in the auditorium when I walked out on the dimly lit stage. I dramatically discarded the pages on the stage.

They sat far in the back, forcing me to give it my all, which I did. Sometimes you know when your future depends on your perfection that moment.

The quality of mercy is not strain'd,
It droppeth as the gentle rain from heaven
Upon the place beneath. It is twice blest,
It blesseth him that gives, and him that takes;
'Tis mightiest in the mightiest; it becomes
The throned monarch better than his crown;
His scepter shows the force of temporal power,
The attribute to awe and majesty,
Wherein doth sit the dread and fear of kings;
But mercy is above this sceptered sway,
It is enthroned in the hearts of kings,
It is an attribute of God himself;
And earthly power doth then show likest God's,
when mercy seasons justice. . . .

Then after a curtsy to show a break in the lines, I performed a second scene, also Portia. This second selection was no doubt given to test my ability to play a boy, which is what I looked like, and which would be an asset in this school of several hundred women actresses and one male student. And so I began in a girl's voice but let myself gently become most manly:

> I'll hold thee any wager,
> When we are both accoutered like young men,
> I'll prove the prettier fellow of the two,
> And wear my dagger with the braver grace,
> And speak between the change of man and boy
> With a reed voice, and turn two mincing steps
> Into a manly stride; and speak of frays
> Like a fine bragging youth; and tell quaint lies
> How honorable ladies sought my love,
> Which I denying, they fell sick and died;
> I could not do withal. Then I'll repent,
> And wish for all that, that I had not killed them;
> And twenty of these puny lies I'll tell,
> That men shall swear I have discontinued school
> Above a twelvemonth. I have within my mind
> A thousand raw tricks of these bragging Jacks,
> Which I will practice.

After these and several other scenes, my two-person audience did not applaud; they talked together for what seemed a very long time and quieter than I could make out. The woman walked slowly toward the stage where I stood motionless—I had gathered up the pages from the floor. The man remained in his seat.

From the foot of the stage she looked up at me: "Do you know how to sew?" she asked. "Come this fall semester we might have a better job for you than Harvard. It would be in our costume department. You could work in the evenings and earn your tuition. We do want you, Doris. We'll find you a good summer job, too, so you'll have your money for board, and some left over for fun."

"I can sew," I replied in a tiny voice, for I knew I could learn.

■ ■ ■

I rushed across the city to set the table for a few hundred young men whom I now pitied for their clay-potted lives. I was floating, soaring, at one with everything royal and sparkling, awake to the miracle of everything. I could see the things of the world now, how the wind and stars worked. I would stare smiling at someone—at them, through them—until they no doubt worried if I were blind or mad or a suicide.

Alan Ayer ducked into the dining hall to see how things had gone. He didn't have to ask; he could tell I was on some opium, and he knew its name was Emerson. He didn't say a thing but just gave me a great smile and a thumbs up. He alone in the grand and wonderful world was sure I could do this thing. I answered him by closing my eyes and sighing with my hands closed over my heart like the great Theda Bara. He waved good-bye from across the room, this lovely man did, and I blew him a kiss that rippled across all the silly little boys staring.

Toward the end of the spring term I had become fairly well ensconced in Harvard life. I had a red-haired Harvard boyfriend—not Alan, alas—who took me to films and to dinner. His father was a state governor out west somewhere. His nickname was Red. His chums in his dormitory teased him endlessly for going to bed with change in his pajama pocket so he could get up and call me first thing. I suppose we petted a bit. Petting only amounted to holding each other close and kissing, though it was pretty nasty stuff coming, as it did, in the face of Victorian sensibilities. There was no fondling below the neck. Some girls and boys were known to go much further, of course, but most of us did not.

Otherwise, our sophistication limited itself to a little gin and an occasional ciggy. There were speakeasy jazz bars where one could go to feel fully in tune with the times. The fact that speakeasies were associated with gangsters, and that Prohibition meant the alcohol there would be dangerously homemade, only made such places the more attractive. I only sipped the gin because my mother had made me promise to stay away from such things, as my eyesight and honor would soon be lost to them otherwise.

Toward the end of the spring term I took a quick trip home by train to hug my family—I was terribly homesick. My career so far in the city, especially my acceptance by Emerson and my arrangements for tuition, was good news to take home. I had returned a roaring success and a big-city sophisticate. I spoke the new flapper slang and knew the latest poses and so-bored eye rolls. I'm sure I must have seemed comical or annoying to my parents, but my sisters hung on my every adventure story.

"Do you spend any time with Alan Ayer?" my father asked. I told him that we saw each other absolutely all the time. It had become less true with each month, but Alan was Father's security blanket, so I kept him in the official story.

The final weeks of the term sped by, and the spring smell of garden mulch perfumed all of Cambridge. The last hidden-away mounds of shaded ice melted across the sidewalks. The Harvard boys headed home to the liveried comforts and well-stocked presumptions of old money, and I packed for Nantucket for a summer as maidservant. Emerson had found me a job in a small inn, the Old Parliament House, run by two women of the island who loved each other quite openly and beautifully.

AT SEA

5

*J*une 1929. The *Nantucket*, a steamer named for its daily destination, carried on the darkened lower deck two dozen grand, gleaming automobiles, creaking back and forth like yachts at evening mooring. Topside, there were long sunny benches of veteran ferry riders—old friends—already in their yellow summer hats and colorful loose cottons. They were all chatting and snacking like in Renoir's *Boat Party*—and then a few seasick people like me.

The trip took several hours, and the seas between Hyannis and Nantucket were rough. Despite my stomach, I was feeling the joy of adventure. I had left the mainland, after all. Far out there somewhere was Ireland, England, France, Spain with its castles—how remarkable! What a planet for adventure! South America was down that way. Africa, roughly there, as I stared across the horizon. The world was wide open to me, fresh and blue and only slightly too bounding.

It was a new iron boat that had very recently replaced the last of the wooden ships serving the Cape and the islands. I was told this and much more by an old man of straw skimmer and jaunty gray moustache and fine blue blazer with brass buttons. He joined me at the rail for some air—no doubt one of the finer automobiles below was his. The Cape itself, and Nantucket and Martha's Vineyard, and many of the ups and downs of New England, he informed me, were created by the gouging action of incoming glaciers and also by the rocks they had picked up during this gouging and had carried along until they dropped into huge piles and islands as the glaciers melted and died. If I'm not mistaken, he was teary-eyed at the thought of it. He composed himself.

"The Laurentide Ice Sheet, to call it by name, Miss, is responsible for most of what you see when you look upon New England and the Cape and the islands. The rocks left behind are called terminal moraines."

His red, weathered face—a sailor's, or rather a yachtsman's face—squinted into a thousand wrinkles as he disclosed these secrets. As I looked at the distant islands on this, my first passage, he swept a hand out to describe the great ice that had come down to do battle.

"Mr. Muir, of the West, writes about how avalanches out there are what he calls part of the beauty-making. Well, Miss, I will put our glaciers up against the West's meager avalanches any day, wouldn't you? Why, the Laurentide had whole mountains for breakfast, and now there is all this beauty to show for it, and not so long ago!" he added.

He could see, glancing downward, that I seemed to have an intelligent body, and so he added a generous bonus of information regarding the fact that the tilt of the earth actually changes over time, helping to cause ice ages when there is not enough warmth at the poles. He went on and on for the rest of the journey, surely saving me from throwing up, as I didn't want to be unladylike in front of him, and so I concentrated mightily and breathed deeply the salt air.

I did not take notes on his geology lecture, by the way, but can reconstruct it because I was soon to meet an amateur geologist who would recount the same story many times.

I went below to seek the ladies' room. I found myself down one level too deep, in the dark of the automobiles. I should have gone right back up the same stairs, but thought I would cut across through the fancy cars and come up on the starboard side. Halfway through the murky maze, I thought I heard a groan in the dark. There was some movement between the cars, like someone stooped down. I rounded the high rear of a luxury limousine and found myself inches from a pale man in a dark coat, perhaps a driver or some kind of guard. Maybe he had dropped something or was checking a tire and was just now standing. He smiled in a rather sick way at my startle. For a second we lurched together with the squeaking cars on the rough sea.

I had just seen the silent film *Nosferatu*, a German import, before leaving Boston. It was my first vampire film. This man in the dark terrified me completely. In the film, a young couple buys a home just across the way from Count Orlok's castle, and blood ensues. The story of how we can become addicted to the life force of others, rather than live our own lives bravely in the light of day, was already an old one, but it was new to me. The film was horrifying and instructive: the young woman had to sacrifice her lovely neck to the Count in order to lure him into the fatal dawn light. What we women do for others during remarkable times would be the theme of the coming decade. But a great many things that year, 1929, would be new to me and to everyone. There was a sense of foreboding already in the darker corners. Popular films, I think, are made popular by their resonance with our mass anxieties. They are thereby predictive. *Nosferatu* had landed in America. He was skulking in the dark alleys of Wall Street and Main Street, watching us, preparing his move.

I bowed several times to the man among the autos and backed away toward the same companionway I had come down. He stood barely visible, like a ghost.

▪ ▪ ▪

The two ladies who owned the Old Parliament House on Nantucket had promised Emerson that, after my daily duties as maid, I would have the time and opportunity to participate in the island's summer theater productions. Until the drama season started, I agreed to run the ladies' big hounds every afternoon along the moor that extended to a point of dramatic surf. I soon learned to trust the hounds off their leashes and run with them very fast and far. I had run races as a younger girl, usually winning against the boys, so this was a comforting return to my youthful superpowers. The summer theater auditions came and went before I realized, and so I did not perform that summer. I did later see one of the plays and was happy to be in the audience and not upon the stage. Running with the big dogs, howling with them and leaping along over the moor was the better show that summer anyway.

My Nantucket adventures were most notable for my spotting a boy from Laconia who was working as a beach lifeguard. I saw him atop his white wood tower with his big arms and chestnut-tan shoulders, all packed like horse flanks in his tank shirt—his dark hair slicked back with seawater. He was big Jim Haddock, two years older and two years ahead of me in high school—the brainy football player who had escaped to Amherst, much to my dreamy admiration.

His binoculars were soon snug to his eyes to better watch my purposefully pathetic swimming strokes between the shore and a platform raft. I was well known for my drama roles back in school, but I was a nobody in his crowd. I wondered if he would even realize that I was someone from home. The bad swimmer was my latest dramatic role, as I was actually a wonderful swimmer.

He was president of his class, number one or two academically, and a big football star in high school. Two other players—brothers quite jealous of him—had jumped him on the practice field and somehow ruined his right knee for sports, except that he still could ski-jump farther than nearly anyone, and had got into Amherst on account of it, and also on account of a local minister who advocated for his scholarship and arranged for some work-study jobs on the Amherst campus. The bad knee would not stop him from exploring thousands of miles of New England mountain trails in later years, by the way, though he was sometimes in pain.

I had not realized how homesick I was until I saw his familiar face. It would have been awkward for me to approach him back home, but in this faraway place we were expatriates, stranded adventurers, and so anything might be possible. I swam past his tower uncounted times with my limping stroke.

Later, there was a public dance on the island, and I saw him across the dance floor. A Nantucket boy I had met earlier in the evening was kind enough, following my exact instructions, to point me out to Jim. I watched through the corner of my eye as Jim shook his head no. Undiscouraged, I walked across the floor and looked up at him.

"I'm from Laconia. You should ask me to dance."

"Is that a rule?"

"Common courtesy. Come on." I led him onto the floor.

During the dance he admitted he had noticed my poor stroke, and he then offered that maybe he could give me some lessons the next day.

I had him.

By the end of summer we were arm in arm and singing to each other the song that had just come out:

You're the cream in my coffee,
You're the salt in my stew;
You will always be . . . my necessity—
I'd be lost without you.
You're the sail of my love boat,

You're the captain and crew;
You will always be . . . my necessity —
I'd be lost without you.

When summer ended he headed back to Amherst, where he was a top student in economics, his chosen vocation, and geology, his true interest. Men did separate their lives into interests and necessities, providing for both. This was done in even the most personal areas of their lives. Women were expected to have but one life, though of course they did not. I was not, by the way, prepared to say good-bye to my redheaded son of a governor at Harvard. It was normal for a girl to have more than one suitor, though common courtesy required a girl to inform her suitors of their rivals, which I did.

Back in Boston, I began my first year at Emerson and started a job I had stumbled across by meeting a wealthy woman staying at the Old Parliament House. She was there to rendezvous with a European man. She was full of fun in other ways, too, and she took a lively interest in my future. She worried about how I would be able to afford "decent" housing in Boston, meaning a grand house, and so she corresponded with her sister in Boston about me.

"We can't have you staying at some dump or the—what is it called? The Franklin Square House?" she had said, referring to the giant apartment hotel for young women.

As it happened, her sister could use someone just like me. I might take the position of "second girl" in a fine summer mansion in Marblehead, overlooking the harbor, and then their regular Boston mansion, not too far from Emerson, right on the Green Line. A second girl is someone who helps the cook serve dinner. This was a notable Boston blueblood family that her sister had married into—Peabody, no less. The job would consist mainly of housekeeping and helping to serve dinner so that Mrs. Peabody—one of many Mrs. Peabodys in New England—might look even wealthier to her almost nightly dinner guests. The Peabodys would provide me with room and board and some spending cash for the year. It was the autumn of 1929—a good moment to have a secure berth, though we hardly realized that yet.

When I returned to Boston after the summer, I had a perfunctory job interview with Mrs. Peabody. She had me meet her at the Ritz

Carlton. She sized me up in about a half minute. She said I should start immediately. The family was presently ensconced just north of town at Marblehead, their summer place on the sea. They would be moving back to town in a few more days. I could help.

She had a grand automobile. It was unusual for women to drive, but she did. We went out to the street and she gracefully slid into the driver's seat. I hopped in beside her from the passenger door. She stared at me.

"You'll ride in the back, Doris," she said most coldly.

I was so offended that, all the way to Marblehead, I answered her many questions about my circumstances, my family, my boyfriend, about Emerson, with one-word answers where possible.

There is a spit of land that divides the sea from the harbor at Marblehead. At the end of the spit reclines a moneyed piece of land with lawns and the mansions of Boston's richest families. The size and elegance of the mansions, and the grand settings, were unbelievable to my working-class eyes. The Peabody estate was on Peach's Point.

"Mr. Peabody wrote a little book about this area," Mrs. Peabody said.

"Oh, he's a writer?"

She did not respond. I may as well have asked if he were a rag picker.

It all went very well. I did my duties well, though life as a domestic servant was awkward for someone as strong-headed and egalitarian as I was. Further, Mrs. Peabody was afraid that Mr. Peabody was a bit taken with me. He may have been, but he was also a gentleman.

I had Jim Haddock fully on my mind. Had that not been the case, I might have been tempted to look at Mr. Robert E. Peabody more closely. Just looking at him, you had to dream a little. I was looking at him out the window one snowy Saturday when he was on his long skis and his wife was beside him on hers. He had been to the North Pole with Peary or something like that, and was a delight to see on his skis—strong, long striding, brilliantly at ease. I was a good skier and was a worthy judge. His wife, however, was so comic beside him that I laughed.

Mary, the Peabodys' cook, was my immediate boss and confidante. She had no business being there at all, as her mother was a successful opera singer, but families are odd.

Mary told me to be very careful, as Mrs. Peabody didn't like the way Mr. Peabody was looking at me. She said that Mrs. Peabody had come from modest circumstances—an innkeeper's daughter at an inn where Mr. Peabody had once stayed—and she surely wasn't going to let go of her fine husband if she could help it. She also said Mrs. Peabody had a famous temper, and had about got the whole household kicked out of the country club up in Marblehead because she was throwing golf clubs around like a wild woman every time she muffed a drive. Mary was very upset that the family was on the blacklist at the club—she took it quite personally.

Mr. Peabody accompanied me on the trolley my first day of classes, just to show me the way. He was very kind and did have the aspect of a trapped man. Away from the house he seemed to change color, inflate a bit, and find his smile. He was full of encouragement about my school year and my eventual career. As a human being he seemed completely switched off at home but fully alive now. I took my leave of him at Copley Plaza, and I waved from the sidewalk as he continued toward Boston Harbor, where he ran a steamship company. Mrs. Peabody saw to it that I found my own way to school the next morning.

Classes were a dream, and I was a natural. The students were, except for one lucky fellow, all girls. We were enjoying life and our youth in a very exciting city.

■ ■ ■

Emerson College was then called Emerson College of Oratory, not because it taught speech, but because it taught communication and how to have a thought worth communicating.

They were serious people. The rocks of Emerson were the Southwicks, husband and wife. Mr. Southwick was descended from the family who had stood their ground against religious intolerance in America. It is nice to think that the early English and Europeans who sailed to America came to advance the cause of religious freedom, but they cared only for religious freedom for themselves, not for others. The Puritan fathers were not above hanging or burning those of other faiths. The Quakers were especially singled out for torture and death. The Southwick ancestors were Quakers, and, when given the choice of recanting their beliefs or dying for their faith, they died for their faith.

Lawrence and Cassandra Southwick of Salem, of whom the generational memory was fresh in the Southwicks I was learning to know, died trying to warm each other in the bitter cold of an island way-station, on their forced journey to an always-short life of slavery in the Caribbean.

Mary Dyer, another Quaker of the same time and place, was hanged to death on Boston Common — not by a mob, but by the ruling Puritan government. She was given a last-minute chance to recant her beliefs or leave the region, but she refused, dying after these words, which greatly moved the crowd observing her death:

> I came to keep blood-guiltiness from you, desiring you to repeal the unrighteous and unjust law of banishment upon pain of death, made against the innocent servants of the Lord, therefore my blood will be required at your hands who willfully do it; but for those that do it in the simplicity of their hearts, I do desire the Lord to forgive them. I came to do the will of my Father, and in obedience to his will I stand even to the death.

This was no mean sacrifice, and the conscience of the future nation was indeed pricked — we owe the Quakers a great deal. So oratory had this aspect with the Southwicks: it is what is said on the scaffold to make a life meaningful, and we are, as mortal creatures, always standing there.

The spot on Boston Common where oratory changed the minds of America's forefathers about religious freedom was well known to us students of the Southwicks'. We knew the spot thirty years before a bronze statue of Mary Dyer was added to the front of the nearby State House.

Some students were at Emerson to learn acting or singing. Some were there to become gentlewomen. Some were there to pass the time. I had come to learn acting, to position myself for that career, but I found myself more moved to learn of Mary Dyer than to read more of Clara Bow in Hollywood.

■ ■ ■

I became something of a procurer. My time at Harvard had put me in regular touch with a number of boys who regularly needed dates. For Emerson students, Harvard boys were good catches. A dinner and movie with a Harvard boy would be something to write home about.

So go ask Dottie. I was the one to see for a Saturday night fix-up. It became a bit difficult to know which of my new Emerson friends actually liked me, and which just liked what I could do for them. There were several girls, however, I thought I could trust with my friendship.

Lulu, something of a gold digger, whom I had met when I first walked into Emerson to apply—she was the receptionist—wasn't exactly friend material but was too full of life not to enjoy having around. She was dark, exciting, full of drama and intrigue—full of gin and sin in ways that my "better" friends would never dare. We were, most of us, flappers on the outside, though quite conventional inside, but Lulu was a flapper through and through, caring only for dangerous moments.

"Butt me, Dottie. Look at that swell guy who just came in. Say, Dottie, you know him, don't you? Look at him, he's so Haaarvard—you must know him. Call him over here so I can ignore him, will you?" She was always bumming smokes.

She used a cigarette holder and was always on full steam. She would drop in and out of my week, usually looking for help, as such people do. My more proper and quite rich friend, Vera, particularly didn't like Lulu and warned that she would be trouble. Actually, they were quite alike, except that Vera was society, so she spun her cynicism into humor, while Lulu was roughly common and spun her cynicism into transparently greedy, usually unsuccessful intrigues.

Lulu sized me up as someone who probably was only good for a few ciggies and an occasional man—though she didn't actually need much help with men. Her orbit was such, and Emerson was small enough, that I could watch her operate. She was, from everything I had read in a thousand magazines, just right for the movies. She was tough enough to do it. So I watched her and darkly admired her, though I collected quite different kinds of people as my closer friends. I think I related to Lulu's modest upbringing. She was a dark role model, whereas Vera was from another world.

For all her charisma and daily drama, Lulu was not the most colorful girl in our circle: that would be Dolores Ramona DeCosta. Ramona—

she went by her dramatic middle name—was brunette, beautiful, and somewhat mysterious. She had big eyes, a movie star smile, and was nicely stacked. She was perhaps Spanish Gypsy by ancestry. Ramona's nose was a little large, but it looked good on her. Her mother, who was as close to her as a sister, had moved to Boston with her two smaller children and no husband. She had done so to support her daughter's career at Emerson. They lived in the most awful tenement in the swampy Fenway, but they were on a serious mission of making Ramona a successful actress. Ramona was a serious person indeed, and she and I recognized that in each other. Her style was uncompromising: she walked and spoke with great dignity. Her dresses were full and colorful, as though the big Gypsy dance were tonight. She was no flapper, but was like a character from one of our Saturday morning plays. She could have had any boy, but she had little time for dates. She was studying, performing, or off with her mother in their other world. She didn't need me in any way, but she liked my company. She felt the weight of her family's future on her shoulders.

Her sense of humor was broad and loud. She would go out for the wilder character parts and usually got them by pushing things over the top. Ramona got the part of a beggar. I got the beggar's daughter, which was the principal role. She didn't care; she wanted the rich characters. I expect that was all strategic: there is never room for more than a few leading actresses in Hollywood or Broadway, but a good character actor can always make a living. Besides, to be a leading actress, you probably needed to be whiter and thinner than she was, and she was a realist.

My taking the best parts became a problem for the sorority types, who knew that I came from modest, unworthy stock and had no right to the choice parts. But someone high at Emerson had her professional eye on me. Many of the girls had enrolled more because Emerson's voice and body studies made it a fine finishing school. But the school did, in fact, produce some serious actors. Somehow, I was the new favorite for serious acting. It hurt when I was turned down for the sorority, but I'm sure they did me a great favor. Over lunch the next day, Ramona, who would never have met their standards either, comforted me with a wave of her long hand: "The world is full of little bitches, Dottie. Don't even think about them. They are nothing to serious people like us. Nothing!" She held her pose rigid in the smoky café until she was sure I understood.

Vera Dealey, the rich one, the one with a convertible automobile, was soon joining us for these little lunches. An Irish-looking redhead, Vera was coolness itself, though not the kind that would get her into a sorority. She drove her expensive convertible and had a kind of joyful contempt for everything staid, for everything establishment. She did not exactly introduce me to the "f" word, but she showed me how it might be used as common punctuation and as a universal adjective. In later years I would recognize her in Dorothy Parker's attitude, and, years after that, in the humor of my friend Molly Ivins.

Vera would go into laughing hysterics, her head on the table and her open hands slapping the wood when hearing about some poor girl's tragic story of love betrayed. "Please!" she would cry for mercy. "Don't these people read books? Don't they know how these things come out? For Christ's sake, it is sad and funny, funny, funny. Shoot me if I fall in love with some callow little ass, will you, dolls?" She would look up plaintively: "Will you please?"

She constantly made up new words and used them as if everyone must know them. A "snorg" was her word for a deadly disappointment. "What a snorg," would be her later review of Herbert Hoover's presidency after so much early excitement. He had rescued children during the Boxer Rebellion and was a good-looking Stanford man with a son at Harvard, so expectations were high.

Vera was as essentially American as Ramona was the exotic, the foreign. I was the wide-eyed, small-town girl watching them—though, as I said, I was getting all the good parts and had the key to the supply closet of Harvard men, so was interesting, too.

Vera thought it was simply hysterical that I was working as a maid to the Peabodys, as if it were a comedy routine of the lowest sort— Laurel and Hardy were the newest laugh.

"Dear God, Dottie, do you prance around in your little maid's costume for Mr. Moneybody? Show us how you pick up something, darling. Dust the legs of that lowboy, will you?" She was relentless.

Bobbie came last. She was a tomboy in the extreme, not much bigger than little me, slim and clearly a flapper by style. You would see her watching our bodies as we visited at the table. We did not consider what that meant, though it is clear in retrospect. She was quick to touch and to empathize, and there was a fierce sense of loyalty about her, as though we might please send her out to do some violent crime for us.

When the Emerson casting calls came up short for a male, which was common, she would take the part and be convincing. If it were a romantic play where she could play against a heroine, she played the love scenes heartbreakingly well.

I worked hard all the time. I worked in the big mansion. I worked in class and on the Emerson stage. I worked mending costumes and organizing the costume department, which paid my tuition. Old Miss Bailey, the costume mistress, had let things get away from her, and I was her angel. We walked the Saturday street markets to find old outfits and new fabrics. Miss Bailey was a little mouse, with a gray bun of hair and very plain looks. It was later a bit of a scandal that she took in and supported a young male dancer, who seemed far too young for her and not inclined toward women. But he had a good supporter in Miss Bailey, who provided for his performance costumes and his housing, and she, in fair exchange, had herself a very good-looking young man for a time.

A Miss Clara Wagner had been her assistant before me, but Clara graduated just as I began at Emerson, and she was now producing costume events for the Boston Parks Department, which was a high responsibility. Boston has a lot of history, and its Parks people produce a great many productions. Clara was considered an Emerson success story. She would drop by to tell Miss Bailey the latest big things happening for her. They were good friends, and so I got to know Clara more and more as they visited. Clara was dark-haired, very stocky and also very plain, but she was so full of creative energy and joy—she may have invented the word "wow"—that you really saw her as quite the thing. Clara arriving always meant the tempo would double—she was the Charleston with her hands high. She was also something of a political revolutionary, which added to her sex appeal. She was one of the best young hostesses in Boston.

When I first started with Miss Bailey, Clara had come by to say hello. She looked at the closetfuls of soiled and torn costumes that had accumulated since she had taken her energy elsewhere, and she gave me a smile and a shrug. It was a "you can do it" gesture. I bravely attacked the great piles.

It was almost defeating. I was a star on the Saturday morning stage, but I became Cinderella just moments after the curtain, as actors tossed their costumes into the department and I was lost to the city and to youth for the rest of the day and evening.

Vera eventually arranged a rescue. They were at our soda fountain, my three friends, feeling sad for my indenture upstairs, when Vera reportedly said, "Oh, damn it to hell, it's no fun without Dottie. Let's go save the little midget."

They came flapping along the upper corridor of the old building like killers, and crashed headlong into the costume department. To Miss Bailey's horror, but soon to her delight, they took up the work, and we finished a day's work in an hour, with loud stories flying that finally caught Miss Bailey up in the mirth. That became the thing they would do after the Saturday morning play, and I was, in that way, freed to have a life.

The four of us—me, Vera, Bobbie, and Ramona—not Lulu, really, who was a solo act—had a plan. We would do Emerson, then move to New York City, get an apartment together, help each other into little plays, then into big ones. We would become a pantheon of Broadway goddesses with lovely apartments on Fifth Avenue.

It was easy to think big, as the autumn of 1929 was shaping up to be a marvelous season. We smoked and laughed when riding in Vera's convertible over to the dances in Cambridge, where I would meet up with Jim, who disagreeably agreed sometimes to dance—perhaps it hurt his bad knee—and where my girlfriends would meet the new princes I had arranged for them. I would find a cynic for Vera, a romantic for Ramona, and a youth of shy disposition for Bobbie—and other men for my other friends. My old days as a Harvard checker girl had made me the most valuable friend a poor girl could have.

I would often see Lulu across a jazz club floor, dancing with someone too young or too old for her, but always he would be well dressed and she would be the shimmering flapper. The styles of the day were superbly dramatic, with bright colors, shiny fabrics, long scarves, cigarette holders, caplike hats, low necklines, high boots flapping open with their laces undone, everything form fitting and drippingly sexy. After a world war there is nothing much remaining to believe in but what may be touched and caressed, folded into wallets, smoked, drunk down, and made love to. We believed in the physical. Enthusiasm was the rite of our religion.

Autos and airplanes and faster trains were providing new freedom, and the career opportunities for young people were endless, here and abroad. The booming stock market was becoming a popular topic of conversation even at lunch counters. The market was not exactly out-pacing baseball as the national pastime, but the steady rise of stocks gave us the idea that prosperity was inevitable. What could stop America now? Nothing. Every one of us could be rich and famous if we just applied ourselves.

The more adventurous young women wanted to become actresses or—the big new thing—airline stewardesses. Those needing fewer thrills might become teachers, nurses, or secretaries. And there might be a rich or at least half-rich husband waiting for every girl who made the effort to snag one. There was no excuse whatsoever for a man not to do well if he had the least bit of get-up-and-go.

Housewives were buying stocks and chatting up steel, automotives, and utilities as a part of everyday conversation.

The expectation of future wealth does give one an attitude. One tends to laugh off stick-in-the mud bosses and landladies. A jazzy dance, a colored ciggy in a long holder, a smashing outfit, a new daddy—these were the things that mattered.

I do not mean to say we did not work hard for our meager pay. We did. But there was a joy that ran under all of us, as if we were wired together and jolted with the same sixty-cycle generator. Andrew Mellon had said that it was "clear sailing" for the economy, and the economy was indeed looking like a yacht. Everybody worth listening to had said positive things. Hoover had been elected and was assurance himself.

Robert E. Peabody was the only person in my daily world who seemed the least bit uneasy about things. I didn't know if he was uncomfortable around me, or if something was bothering him more generally, perhaps his marriage.

On an evening when Mrs. Peabody was away at her family home in Vermont, and when Mary, the cook, had already gone to bed, I was reading a school textbook in Mr. Peabody's library—something I would never have dared do with Mrs. Peabody in the house, as servants were to clean such rooms but not enjoy them. Mr. Robert Peabody, however, did not mind in the least and told me so one evening when he saw me studying in the kitchen. He was a great student of things himself, and so appreciated having a warmly lit, private space for opening a new book and letting one's imagination off its leash. He was a fine writer, by the way—it ran in his family. Rather on the sly, I would read things he and his forebears had written—I would notice them and even look for them as I cleaned and straightened his library. Also I noticed how respectfully but confidently he held and carried the books of his household—he nearly always had one in hand—which made me want to take care of them all the more.

He now stood in the draped doorway long enough for me to sense that he was there. He had something to say but was hesitating.

He was very good looking with strong features, tall, built like a seaman, with black curly hair, big hands, and intense eyes. He seemed quite old to me but was barely forty. I had a natural sympathy for him, perhaps because he looked like he would make a good father, yet he was childless. They once had a beautiful son, who died in his crib. Mrs. Peabody's often-uncontrollable anger was something I worried about in connection with that. And Mary, the cook, whose bedroom was in the half-story attic above their bedroom and who was addicted to listening at a steam pipe hole in the floor, told me pathetic stories of how he begged her to have another child, but she always refused him the necessary intimacy. So I was immensely sympathetic to him. I knew he must have incredible needs. I really thought he should toss her overboard and start life again.

Whether or not he had the necessary cruelty to do it would be the question. There was a promising hint of the rogue in his looks, which came by him naturally. Most of America's first big-money families, including his, got their fortunes by sailing fleets of semi-pirate ships— privateers—that preyed upon the ships of nations unfriendly to the new American colonies. I say "semi" because piracy was but a lucrative sideline to their otherwise more ordinary business of maritime trade. There were also the other kind of pirate ships roaming the seas, whose only trade was piracy, and who answered to no government or law or code of decency. Privateers, however, operated with the permission of the colonial governments and later the American government itself. Perhaps they were more genteel than pirates per se, but their canons, muskets, and swords were no kinder to a victim's health.

It is interesting how so little changes over the centuries. Privateering now finds its harbor on Wall Street and in the banks, but it is the same principle: the official protection of theft. The fortunes still pile up—often in the same old families.

Robert E. Peabody ("E" for Ephraim) was in fact the great-great-grandson of Elias Hasket Derby, owner of a square-rigged shipping fleet, a privateer, and America's first millionaire.

Robert was himself a seaman. When I met him he was dry of all that and well ensconced on land as the son of a world-famous architect. Nevertheless, he had sailed across the Atlantic after graduating Harvard in '09, and then became the assistant purser of a ship called the *Esperanza*, which traveled between New York, Havana, and Mexico continuously. When I knew him, he was managing supplies for the Emery Steamship Company, operating over two hundred vessels out of Boston Harbor. He had worked his way up the shipping business from an office boy in the New York docks, though he needn't have worked at all.

Robert was also a noted maritime historian who wrote *Log of the Grand Turks* and *Merchant Venturers of Old Salem*, as well as a history of the Derbys, and other maritime biographies, textbooks, and articles. He helped promote and endow the family's maritime museum in Salem, which, since 1799, had grown its extraordinary collection of anthropological and natural history artifacts by recruiting every New England sea captain to bring back curiosities from around the world.

Robert's nose was bred through many generations to sniff incoming weather, and he rather now smelled the Depression coming. There were no helpful facts involved, just the scent of it.

"Doris," he began, "you're doing a good job, and I'm going to increase your money by a little—not much: a token, really, to show we appreciate you."

I thanked him very much, but could see there was some condition tumbling slowly my way.

"You know, Doris, there are some troubling things going on in the economy lately. You aren't one of these people who puts every dollar into the stock market, are you?"

He lit his pipe and waited for my answer. My every dollar had gone to my daily survival. He should have known that, but such people, if they respect you for any reason, assume you must have family money somewhere. They simply don't understand the concept of not having money. When you are with them, they will, out of cardboard courtesy, try to keep the strange facts about your circumstances in their heads for as long as they can. But then it will slip away, and they will ask you where your family summers, or they will add a "how about you?" to the end of some long opinion about the relative advantages of the French Mediterranean over the Italian. In fairness, there's very little else they know enough to talk about, so they are bound to slip up.

I told him that I put any spare dollars into my education. He approved with a stern nod. I could see more coming.

"Here's the other thing. I would like you to do me a special favor. Mrs. Peabody is away, so this is a good time for us to talk. It has been on my mind."

I may have stiffened a bit. I hoped my meager raise hadn't come with the extra duty I was afraid he might next propose. If not afraid, I was at least excited.

"There is something I need for you to do for me, but of course it will be our little secret—Mrs. Peabody wouldn't appreciate knowing about it."

I squeezed closed my textbook and my knees and sat with all the dignity I could muster. One thinks about where one might spend the night if one has to bolt into the street. But would I bolt? He looked like a great pirate captain in the rosy light of the paneled room, now grown small. A spiral hook of pipe smoke curled into the space between us.

"You see, the expense of running this house is quite large, as I'm sure you can imagine. Mrs. Peabody likes the house to look well-lighted and prosperous, but I would like to ask you to turn off as many electric lights as possible, except in the front rooms—if you would be so kind. Just a little secret between us, as the electric rates are becoming a very big item, really. I don't want Mrs. Peabody to worry about such things, and I know she doesn't want the house to look dark and deserted, you see? But if there are some changes coming to business conditions, and I think there are, then it is a good time to reef the sails a bit, cut down on waste."

"Yes, of course. That is what you wanted to ask?"

"Yes." He looked straight at me—he just stared for a moment and puffed smoke like a steamship.

How was it that I felt disappointed? Was my presence in the household not torturing him at all? I said I would do as he asked, and I thanked him again for the raise. He nodded and disappeared, leaving his smoke. I was so pleased with myself for not blurting out, "but I am a virgin," which I had come close to saying as a shield against his advance. I wondered if he would have laughed—or would he have been sympathetic to such a faux pas? Perhaps both. I laughed at myself when I later realized that such a man, even if his wife would not have him in her bed, had all the women he needed down nearer his palatial, white-pillared (and still now standing) office at 114 State Street—near Faneuil Hall in the harbor. Or he perhaps had companionship in the private rooms of the Harvard Club or the Union Boat Club, where he was, of course, a member. Surely he had no trouble, this seagoing grandson of a privateer whose very name was the favored New England synonym for Money.

BUBBLES BURST

6

*O*ctober 1929. It was on account of Robert E. Peabody and my devotion to him and to the secret we shared, such as it was, that I may have caused some trouble for absolutely everyone, or so I once worried.

La Seville was a Spanish-themed restaurant owned by the Ginter family, well-regarded Boston restaurateurs. It was located prominently on Boylston at Tremont, across from Boston Common. We girls sometimes went there for a fancier lunch than could be provided by the little lunch counter downstairs from Emerson, or by the Tobey House beanery in Copley Square. We went all the way down to the La Seville whenever Vera wanted to take us out for something decent. She had money, and she grew tired of the grub we otherwise ate. Though La Seville had Spanish decor, the menu was American. It was always full of loud politicians from the State House across the Common, accompanied by their svelte secretaries or by gangster-cool lobbyists. Mousy male bureaucrat staffers huddled at their own tables, their heavy souls lost in gray furrows, while the politicians and others had long ago auctioned theirs off and were lighter now of load and clearer of intentions.

The four of us were probably always a loud table, but Vera tipped well, and so we were always welcomed by the elderly waitress who seemed to rule the place and who would one day be my boss there. On one of our visits, mid or late October 1929, there was another table even louder than ours, even louder than the politicians: three men — two were obviously bureaucrats and the third was a well-heeled lobbyist or executive of some kind — were arguing about the local electrical utility company. The expensively dressed man was arguing for some kind of approval for something. The two others were taking a hard line against it. They first came to our attention when one of the bureaucrats knocked over his water glass when repeating, "you're milking! I say milking the rate-payers."

Vera, Bobbie, and Ramona may have noticed that I then kept losing my place in our conversation because I was eavesdropping. I couldn't make sense of it, but it kept drawing me in, and I was thinking of my promise to Robert E. Peabody to do something about the electric bill. They may not have been talking about that subject at all, but it seemed so, perhaps because it was on my mind.

I was coming back to the table from the ladies room when I passed the men, leaving. I smiled and said, "Stand up for the people," or some such thing. They looked confused but smiled and let me pass.

I told the girls what I had done. They laughed, Vera most of all. I said that if the Peabodys were having a hard time with their electricity bill, it must be a terrible problem for others. Ramona said it wasn't a problem in their tenement, as they didn't have a lick of it. Vera and Bobbie were not of an age or circumstance to care about such things.

Anyway, I would come to regret making the remark to the men.

The reason for that regret is as follows: It is well known that several Boston bureaucrats were in a rather bad mood one day when Boston Edison asked permission to have its stock split, four new shares for every present share. Companies do that to keep their stocks affordable to smaller investors. Say you have one hundred shares of Boston Edison valued at one hundred dollars per share. If they split the stock by four, you will have four hundred shares at twenty-five dollars each. It will be the same to you, but the stock will be easier to trade on the exchanges, and stocks usually go up when they split, as it is a sign that management expects further rises.

But Boston's electric rates were about twice what the people of Cambridge paid, just across the Charles. The people of Cambridge owned their own generators. Was Boston Edison's stock doing so well, needing to be split, because the company was taking Boston citizens to the cleaners? Some men in government thought so, and from their offices near the margins of Boston Common, they refused to allow the stock split. There were suggestions by the same officials that the utility might please look at its rates before trying again. They even suggested that perhaps the City of Boston should provide its own electricity to the people, as some other towns did. All this came right after a noted British expert had said that American stocks were terribly overpriced. They probably weren't—at least by historical standards. Even with all the buying, stocks were mostly valued from ten to twelve times their annual earnings, which is not unusually high. Just the same, the market had become less a means of financing business expansion, and more a no-lose casino. But everyone knows that nothing lasts forever, and so mass anxiety builds. The press picked up the idea that stocks were overvalued, and nervousness set in. Hoover had been privately alarmed about the level of speculation.

The chairman of the new Federal Reserve had been saying for some time that stocks were too high. He had begun to tighten the money supply, hoping that people would stop borrowing money to buy stocks. But investor exuberance was probably not altogether irrational, given the prospects for growth. The thing that seemed to upset some elite leaders was the fact that regular people were buying in. The slaves were buying the plantation! That, coming only a decade after the revolution in Russia, must have looked absolutely un-American to some at the top. But all measures to restrain the market were not working.

There was one sector of the market that was indeed overvalued, and that was the utility stocks. They were odd birds, as often a utility would be purchased by a holding company, which would then be purchased by another holding company, and each transaction would include a good bit of borrowed funds to make the purchase. So these things were teetering in a way that a small contraction of the money supply, which increases loan rates, or a small drop in profitability, as would happen if a city decided to make its own electricity, could collapse things pretty quickly. It was very much the same thing that was to happen in the first decade of the 2000s with packaged and repackaged home loans.

At any rate, the Boston Edison stock took a tumble when the bureaucrats disallowed the stock split as a punishment for its high electric rates in Boston. The whole utility sector followed Boston Edison downward, and then the whole market crashed. The Boston events were considered by some to be the trigger of the stock market crash that brought on the Great Depression, although there are as many theories as to what caused the crash and the Depression as there are historians and economists. Certainly the Federal Reserve gets the blame, rightly, for letting the little banks fail, rather than coming to their rescue with cash guarantees to stop the panic withdrawals. Some thought that the big bankers on the Fed's board of governors were happy to see the smaller banks — their competitors — fail. Some thought they were happy to see stock prices fall, so they could buy up companies at deep discounts, which they indeed did. At any rate, stocks collapsed, "margin" loans made to investors were called due by their brokers, and the Fed didn't make enough money available to refinance those loans. Runs began on banks; the Fed stood and watched; businesses began to lose the credit they needed to buy things and to pay people and stay open. So it all fell down.

I knew a girl back in Laconia — a lovely dancer — whose father killed himself over the losses of that first week. "The coward!" my father wrote to me. But I don't know if he was a coward. His daughter was able to attend college on his life insurance money. When a soldier falls upon a hand grenade to save the futures of his comrades we call it courage, not cowardice. I don't know what it was, but I am not quick to judge what people do in tough circumstances.

Either way, a suicide was remarkable news, as that sort of thing was not much done. There is enough grit in the character and lithium in the water of the Granite State to keep most of us bumping along through the toughest of times, and the solid sense of community is its own safety net. So this was a scandal.

Shocks such as this were all in the news and in conversations. City life in Boston, however, looked no different for a time. Then, everything began to slow down. There were fewer people in the restaurants, more people in soup lines, and it just got worse and worse over the coming months and years. You wondered how bad it might get — there didn't seem to be a bottom.

I picked up as much from the news as I could understand in those first days after the crash. I attempted to explain it all to Bobbie, Ramona, and Vera over our drugstore lunches — I was sometimes repeating what I had learned from Jim, my fancy economist boyfriend who took the train east from Amherst on the weekends to visit me. Ramona was predisposed to think the world was a hard place, so the falling dominoes of the economic crash and depression were as natural to her as falling autumn leaves.

"In a hundred years we'll laugh about it," she said.

Bobbie was saddened by the spiraling down of the economy and of life, pointing out sad people on the sidewalks. She was sure people were sadder than last month. Sometimes she had tears in her eyes to see a family or an old fellow on the sidewalk in hard times, and I realized that she was the most genuinely empathetic of any of us. We all gave pennies and nickels sometimes, but a nickel was actually a lot of money for us. Vera was the richest but never could part with a nickel for a stranger, other than for waitress tips, which were earned, not begged. She used her cynicism and wit as a wall between herself and humanity.

In conversation, Vera could look at you like she was very interested and getting it all. But you never knew exactly what she was thinking. It usually turned out to be quite simple and was about something regarding that next Saturday. She blew off the crash and the worsening Depression.

"It's your fault anyway," she would say, referring to my run-in with the men in the restaurant, which had been magnified into our joke.

Thanksgiving of 1929 was not much of a Thanksgiving for anybody. It was my first Thanksgiving away from home, and most of my school friends were not in the city. I had to work over the holiday for the Peabodys, so there I was. A very kind Harvard boy took me out for a turkey dinner, but I broke down crying in the middle of it.

7

JIM'S GIRL

*M*y second spring in Boston found me still smiling to passersby on the sidewalks, though less generously. The city had worked its way into me, and I was aware of things I would not have noticed a year earlier: a scholarship boy on a Cambridge sidewalk could easily be distinguished by his demeanor from a wealthy boy; an employed man, secure of mind, could be distinguished from even the best-dressed job seeker. The layers of the city were settling in my eyes.

My plans for a future of acting seemed less exciting but more inevitable—I was on an assembly line now, with parts in plays and new little talents added to me like the pinstriping and hubcaps on a new phaeton.

My routines of work and study were daunting, but I trudged through it. I worked in the costume department, I attended classes, I secured and performed parts in the flood of plays produced by Emerson, and I served and cleaned for the Peabodys. I was looking forward to the relaxing labors of my coming summer job, in the same place as the previous summer in Nantucket.

Before leaving Boston for passage to the island, I let the Peabodys know I would not be returning in the fall. Mr. Robert E. Peabody shook my small hand with both his and wished me a great career. I was shocked at how rough and strong his hands were. I thought of him as a writer, but of course he had been a sailor, too, and his business at the harbor was certainly not all paperwork. Mrs. Peabody glared and added no additional good wishes to his.

I left their employ because Lulu had suggested I dump that curtsied drudgery for something more fun, like a waitress job with her at La Seville, where I could flirt with boys endlessly and make more money to boot—even after the new expense of my own apartment. My Nantucket experience serving meals was sufficient reference for La Seville. Lulu suggested I get an apartment at the Franklin Square

House apartments for women, where they had private parlors for boy-friends to come visit. That was where she lived.

■ ■ ■

Nantucket 1930 proved a fine summer. Jim and I swam and danced. We necked and petted in the shadows. I ran the hounds to the sea and back and met interesting guests. The ladies of the Old Parliament House seemed to want to just adopt me, and they liked Jim, too.

I had made arrangements for Ramona to have a job with me in the little hotel, so it was all lovely—though the work in the kitchen and flipping mattresses and doing laundry was hard. Ramona was so funny that summer; the two ladies of the Old Parliament loved her. She wasn't as easily pushed around as I, and they were in awe of her big Gypsy presence and color. She moved always in a dance, and these women loved to watch a woman move. Ramona became the star of the Nantucket community dances. People stopped dancing to watch her, and she laughed her head back whenever she made a great move.

Autumn came quickly, and the three of us walked to the boat, a happy lifeguard and his two flapper girlfriends. From their porch, the two ladies of the Old Parliament wished us a happy school term and invited us all back again next summer.

Jim returned to Amherst for his senior year. I checked into the Franklin Square House apartments. The building was, and remains, a city-block-square, eight-story-high, elegant feature of the city. It has had many lives, built originally as the St. James Hotel where President Grant once stayed—I doubt he stayed in my small room.

After thirty years as a hotel, and still before my time there, it be-came the New England Conservatory of Music, where Jessie Eldridge, later Jessie Eldridge Southwick, my teacher at Emerson, lived and studied. Tuition back then was five dollars a semester, she told us. The noise of the new elevated railway forced the conservatory to move to quieter quarters. In my time, thanks to the leadership of a local min-ister, it had become the largest hotel for working girls in the country and perhaps the world. It survived a fire in 1909 that sent some girls to the hospital, but otherwise was safe and well regarded—except by the wealthy elite of the city, who disdain all things connected with necessity. There were six hundred or more of us dreaming our dreams there every night. It had cheap but good meals, a library, salons for visiting, a sewing and ironing room, and very kindly and wise women running it. We looked out our windows at Franklin Square Park, where, more and more, people who had become newly homeless were sleeping.

The building featured a grand ballroom, with curtained alcoves all around it. A girl could sit in an alcove to visit her boyfriend, but the ladies on duty would come around, looking enough under the curtains to see that four feet were on the floor.

The building has kept its good looks and had a role even late in life as the exterior for the television program *St. Elsewhere*, if I might digress.

Jim would come visit me there most Saturdays, but the alcoves weren't quite what he was hoping for. On a fevered cold evening, we rented a hotel room under the elevated train and enjoyed a few hours in each other's arms. We did not make love, but the intimacy was sweet, and I think we knew we wanted to be with each other forever after that. At the end of weekends I would walk him back to his train and then miss him terribly as I walked home alone.

I thought a lot about sex. I wanted to try it. My friends and I joked about sex, of course; we acted cool and jazzy and urban—we didn't mind if we heard something off-color about someone's adventure—but for most of us, nearly all of us, a girl's body was Fort Knox, and the only way past her buttons was through the front door of a wedding chapel.

I returned to Laconia for the holiday break of that year, 1930—my sophomore year. That visit was a treat, as I did not get holidays off the previous year, with the Peabodys.

My father had purchased an old rattling Model T from a friend in desperate circumstances, and he honked the horn as we traveled home from the Laconia train station. An article had just run in the local newspaper about how I was appearing in a Boston play. He wanted everyone to see that I was back in town and riding in his car. My mother was speechless with joy through the weekend, as her dreams of family stardom were ever so much closer.

December 28, 1930: Miss Doris Rollins of this city and a sophomore at Emerson College of Oratory is appearing in the dramatization of Mrs. Dwight Morrow's story, "The Painted Pig" which will be produced in Boston. "The Painted Pig" is an old Mexican legend hitherto almost unknown in America. Count Rene O'Harnoncourt, the well-known Austrian artist, is cooperating in the dramatization. Miss Rollins was a graduate of Laconia High School in 1927 where she took a prominent part in the high school dramatics and activities.

The New Year was celebrated calmly, as the Depression was settling in and people no longer could see a quick recovery. My triangle of travel between Emerson, La Seville Restaurant, and Franklin Square House took me past a number of desperate soup kitchens. Some of the men would give me a hard time, but most were too sad—too newly poor and still in shock—to do more than smile meekly as I passed. I smiled back, of course, being from a small town. It was frightening at night, however, so sometimes I wasted a dime on the subway to feel safer.

■ ■ ■

Lulu's more-sporting life, and the culture of the working girls at Franklin Square House, presented a new world to me—I resisted being drawn into it too thoroughly. The Emerson of Jessie Eldridge Southwick, whose fine home we students sometimes visited, was a heavy keel to keep me upright in those waters.

I had less and less time for Vera, Bobbie, and Ramona. It is true that everyone was becoming more serious, but even beyond the change of atmosphere that descended with the Depression, they thought I was shunning them. So I tried harder to find the time and money for our lunch-counter visits. Vera was now on a tight budget from her family, who had done the remarkable thing of selling her car and thereby sending her into a permanent gloom—her humor turned acid. She stopped coming to La Seville as often, as did the other girls. Many of my gent friends from Harvard did come, however, and I gave them extra-large ice cream desserts—the rich do very well in hard times and get extra scoops of everything. At first this excess was a problem with the management, but it became clear that I had brought in a rather large, new, and big-spending crowd, so the ice cream flowed.

I only had time for Jim now. I hadn't gone out with another boy in months. The last other date I could remember was right after the holidays when a skinny Harvard boy picked me up at Franklin Square in his car and took me to a speakeasy. It was my first time in a bootleg gangster bar. The place was on Boylston, upstairs and across from a theater. I enjoyed the modest show and sipped my drink carefully. He, however, downed one gin after another.

On the way home, he nearly passed out while driving.

"You take the wheel, Dottie, and I'll drive." I didn't know what that meant, but I turned the wheel this way and that while he flopped around working the gas and the brakes and the shifter. I said we had better head over the bridge to Harvard and to his apartment in Somerville, because if he dropped me off at Franklin Square he could never get home by himself. So we did that. I steered his contraption back and forth along the streets and over the bridge, and after several years of that, we were in front of his rooming house. I turned off the key, and he fell asleep right there. I walked the forever way home, arriving in the frightening dark of early morning. It was easy to say no to others after that. I decided I was Jim's girl, anyway.

The winter melted, and soon Jim and Ramona and I were once again in the thick yellow Eden of a Nantucket summer. It was special, as Jim had graduated Amherst with high honors and, after the summer job, would be moving to Boston to begin a career.

He hadn't asked me the big question, but it was hanging in the atmosphere of each evening like a great comet. He of course wanted to secure a position first, which was only proper.

After the summer, which was fine and a healthy time away from the Depression's disintegration of normal life on the mainland, the boat trip back to Boston felt heavy.

Jim rented a small apartment in Boston where he might begin searching for a job with a bank. He had graduated with an economics degree and a geology degree and had glowing letters from his professors. He expected to find something despite the problems of the economy. To pay his rent and his meals, he took a job at the corner bookstore across from the South Meeting House — the bookstore is still there. He was mostly moving books between the store and the trains at North Station, receiving shipments and sending out customer orders. He pushed a cart along the sidewalk for much of the workday, ducking into corners when he saw his classmates on the street, and dropping off job applications at offices along the way. He would visit me a couple times each week.

On Saturday nights Jim and I would talk and kiss in a ballroom alcove at Franklin Square. He was not much on dancing, so our alcove was checked often by the ladies. He was always a reluctant dancer, and not much of one, but I loved to be held by him on the dance floor.

The managers at La Seville were happy to see me back as I began my junior year. Lulu had worked the summer at the restaurant but was not the favorite there, as she had a reputation for coming late and forgiving too many items on the checks in order to engineer higher tips.

She seemed to feel abused by my popularity with management. She made up for this by dating as many customers, waiters, cooks, and busboys as she could manage. I was somewhat scandalized by her rumored promiscuity, but we were friends, and I liked the fact that she would often be available to walk the long way back to Franklin Square through the hardening neighborhoods — saving me a dime fare.

The gloom of the economy was now a stench of fear on every nighttime street. I was glad to have Lulu walking with me, as she was fearless and loud, and no one bothered us.

"You know that little shy fella who comes in?" We were walking fast in the cold along Tremont, and she was referring to a Harvard boy named Danny. "Can you fix me up with him? I can't get him to even look at me when I serve him. But I think he's cute."

He was not cute. I was feeling less and less honorable about fixing her up — feeling more like a procurer and less like a friend. She had no business with a boy like Danny, really. He was a baby — very sweet, very introverted, very pink-cheeked, and very rich. That was the thing for Lulu. Danny's father had a big string of jewelry stores in New England and New York, and everybody knew it, especially Lulu. But I looked at her chugging along beside me with great clouds of smoke and breath in the frozen night and I felt that maybe someone truly nice like Danny could do her some good. I agreed to talk to him.

Some days later I sat down with Danny as he finished his extra-large dessert and suggested he do a favor for me in regard to Lulu, who needed a date on Saturday and "was too shy to ask." Would he please be a prince? A gentleman would of course agree to be of service if not otherwise engaged.

Then I put the matter out of my mind, and months rolled by. I had my job to do organizing the costumes that year for Emerson's huge children's theater project. I was truly on the run all day and night.

On a Friday, the day before Halloween, many of the students arrived in costumes just for fun — I was a puppy. I was rushing down an Emerson hallway when I encountered Ramona dressed as Stravinsky's firebird. She stopped me with Gypsy murder in her eyes. Her dark eyes and deep voice and the angry wag of her feathered head were intense:

"Dottie. You need to talk to your friend Lulu. I can't say why." All the inflections of Expressive Oratory and the use of costumed wings were perfected in her.

I couldn't imagine what it was, and I didn't see Lulu all day. She was skipping classes. But she appeared for her shift at the restaurant that night. She was tense and maybe a little tight, and she wouldn't look at me. We worked through the shift, then I cornered her on the sidewalk as we left. I broke her easily into tears.

"You don't know what's wrong with me?" she asked through sobs.

I did not. She brightened.

"Exhaustion. Nervous exhaustion. I think I may have a breakdown," she said, almost cheerily now, as though she just thought of it and it sounded wonderful.

"I need to get away. I need to find a place far from here, far from my family, and just rest and read a book, or I think I may just kill myself."

She then resumed crying. I put my arms around her, and we leaned against the alley wall. I was exhausted too, so I understood. And I had a plan.

"We can put you on a train in the morning. You can have my bed back home for a week. My sister is still living at home, and she is studying to become a nurse. She can practice on you. You can read and drink tea, and come back good as new."

She cuddled into me.

"That sounds too good to be true."

Our home had recently installed a telephone, which I called that evening to talk with Mother and my sister. They were agreeable. The next morning, I put Lulu on the northbound Boston & Maine.

THE BOHEMIANS

8

A week later I received a letter from my sister Sybil. She told me what she could not have said on the party-line telephone, that Lulu had come to out-of-the-way Laconia to abort a pregnancy. The letter shook in my hand.

I did not keep the letter over the years, as it was so shameful, but here it is as I remember it, and I would wager it is not ten words off. I read it a hundred times, after all, even as I walked down the sidewalk so intent with it and angry that I did not even look up to scowl at the whistlers in the soup lines:

> I caught her taking some terrible poisons and she confessed every-thing to me. A busboy at the restaurant, it seems, got her in the family way. Mother found out and is furious. I told Mother that nobody is perfect, and we owed the girl a Christian bed until she was well enough to travel. Mother has agreed to this, but through her teeth, I'll say! What's worse, and Mother does not know this, but Lulu confessed that she blamed her pregnancy on some nice boy at Harvard—his name is Danny—and she got some money from his father! Isn't that awful? Someone should tell him. Do you know him? Anyway, she is good practice for me, so I will do my best.

Lulu was not in class for a full week, but I knew from other girls at Franklin Square House that she was back in Boston. I finally overcame my anger and knocked on her door. Lulu had indeed taken care of her situation. She confessed the entire thing. At a soda fountain, on the night after she had told me she was having a nervous breakdown, Danny's father, a seething, stone-quiet man wearing a Jewish yarmulke, had personally delivered the money to her so she would please disap-pear. By her private treachery, she had made his family her scapegoat. Civilizations and empires enlarge what we do personally. There was a horror of scapegoating yet to come in these awful times.

Regarding her method of taking care of things: In those days, there were often newspaper and magazine advertisements, usually small ads in the back, promoting various female tonics to "restore" health that "should not be taken when pregnant," or, the ad warned, spontaneous abortion would result. This, of course, was the whole point of those "remedies." Whether or not they worked was another matter—no buyer could complain without exposing her true intent. Other methods were also common, including flushing with high-pressure water and, of course, the use of instruments. About one in four pregnancies in the 1920s resulted in abortion. About one in six abortions resulted in death: the same odds as Russian roulette with a six-shooter. I don't know what Lulu did, but she did it in my home in Laconia, with my nurse sister in the next room, and she had done this thing with a damnable lie to a nice fellow and his family.

She looked awful. She had just been visited by a doctor who gave her some sulfa drug and told her she would be all right. There were no such things as antibiotics yet, so it was always the flip of a coin whether you would overcome an infection or it would overcome you.

I so deeply regretted having sent her to my wonderful home and my brilliant, warmly caring nurse sister, Sybil. Father had even met Lulu at the train. In thinking back, I realized that Lulu had led me to suggest the whole thing. I thought it was my idea that she should go to Laconia, but she had manipulated the conversation with little hints.

Mother was terribly mad at me for having such friends, and it would cause her to reject me later when I most needed her. Mostly I was mad at myself. I wanted to get out of Franklin Square House and far from Lulu.

I told her, by the way, that if she did not tell Danny the truth, I would. She agreed, and I knew later that she did.

■ ■ ■

It has often been the case in my life that when I was intent on doing the right thing, a door opened. I was working my costume job at Emerson when Clara Wagner came in for one of her courtesy calls to Miss Bailey. She came in often enough, sharing her success stories and helping us for an hour or so of making a new costume or making repairs. She and I had become almost friends during these visits. This particular visit, she found Miss Bailey not in attendance. Miss Bailey was at a recital watching her gentleman friend dance.

So Clara helped me sew a child's costume. She added an imaginative leafy collar while I told her my story about Lulu. I should have kept it to myself, but it was all over school anyway, and I just couldn't hold it in. I had to talk to somebody about it. Jim wouldn't want to hear about that sort of thing, and Vera, Ramona, and Bobbie already criticized me for even knowing Lulu.

Clara listened and looked wise.

"I have an idea," she said. She had found an angle in it for herself, and a way out for me.

"Right across Boston Common from that restaurant where you work, right up behind the capitol buildings, there are those great apartments on Beacon Hill. You know where I mean?"

I knew where Beacon Hill was, of course, but I thought it was all blueblood rich families. There are mansions along most of the streets and around Louisburg Square on the side facing the river and Cambridge across the water. But, Clara explained, there were fairly cheap apartments along Joy Street, a good mix of things.

"I was looking up there the other evening," she went on, "and there's a place for rent, if it still is, that I just love. But I would need a roommate to take half the rent. Do you want to look at it? It would save you a lot of walking and subway fares, and the people there are amazing artists and whatnot. There are parties almost every night. The Boston Symphony practices almost next door. Think of it! And it's right near the Boston Common, which is where many of my events are, so it will be convenient for both of us. No more train fares for you!"

My share of the rent would be about three dollars a week, about the same as I was paying at Franklin Square. That's still a lot of money if you're earning twenty-five cents an hour and have to eat and go to school.

"I don't even have to see it," I replied. "Let's do it!" I knew her taste was impeccable, and she would not have picked a dump. Even so, who would be better to fix a place up? Moving from Lulu's world to Clara's world was not an occasion for hesitation—it would perhaps even set me up for jobs with her later. And I knew Jim would love the privacy of it.

By the next Sunday, I was out of Franklin Square House and had become a new resident of Joy Street. The landlord of our building, the self-described King of the Joy Street Fairies, was a gloriously dressed, big, loud, gay man who said we should please let him host a welcome party. I had fallen into the most interesting neighborhood in America, with a Jewish roommate, a reigning King, and a multiracial, multi-everything cast of characters. Only a short walk from the park grove where Mary Dyer had been hanged for being but slightly different, freedom had come to America—with empathy, mutual appreciation, and creative encouragement as the only rules of behavior. Joy Street was where runaway slaves had come before the Civil War. It was the first racially integrated neighborhood in America. The Park Street Church at the bottom of the hill—it is still there—was where William Lloyd Garrison had preached the beginnings of the abolition movement that led to war and emancipation. Women's rights had an important address on Joy Street, as did gay and lesbian freedom. It was one of the bohemian centers of the continent—a tiny Paris. Greenwich Village was of course thriving in New York City, and its avant-garde inhabitants would reshape the nation's artistic sensibilities, just as the avants of New Orleans would reshape our music. But Joy Street's freethinkers would reshape our political sensibilities and our rights.

Clara was an unstoppable entertainer. I would almost run home from my evening job at La Seville to see who was there and what was happening. Clara bloomed up colorfully in the confidence of her own element. She was introducing me to people and issues I did not dream even existed. I somehow managed to do my schoolwork, too.

An old piano that came with the apartment was Clara's favorite spot: she played beautifully and she played jazz, belting out "Barney Google with the Goo-Goo-Googly Eyes" and singing with a laughing voice.

The apartment included a big room with windows opening onto a garden on Joy Street, screened by a little wall. There was one bedroom and a small kitchen. There was an old tapestry on the wall of the front room—a jungle scene with a tiger in deep shadows. Clara and I both knew enough William Blake to recite the great tiger poem:

Tiger, tiger, burning bright
In the forests of the night,

What immortal hand or eye
Could frame thy fearful symmetry?

In what distant deeps or skies
Burnt the fire of thine eyes?
On what wings dare he aspire?
What the hand dare seize the fire?

"That poor tiger," Clara said one evening. "What's he doing on Beacon Hill, do you suppose? Don't you think he needs a proper jungle?"

Her idea was to paint the whole room like a jungle. The landlord King, after a few gins, heartily approved. Clara had me summon half the art students from Harvard to come execute the grand mural over a weekend. It was a jungle with monkeys in the trees, snakes wrapped around branches, a jaguar peeping out — all in bright greens with huge, red flowers. It was a sensation. The project established our little apartment as the place to come for chats and a ciggy, and sometimes one might bring a little gin. Politics and the economy were debated and solved almost nightly. On the night the mural was declared finished, Lulu showed up.

"I heard about it. I wanted to see it. She looked past me in the doorway to the mural and the people. Clara joined me at the door. I made the introduction coldly.

"Oh, of course," Clara said, "You're Dottie's dear friend," and she offered her hand.

"Do come in and have a closer look," she said to Lulu. "Let me get you an ashtray. Do you drink, dear?" And, with that, Lulu was back in my life, though just as an occasional visitor in a busy living room. We understood each other, and were intent on getting on with our lives. I did admire her in many ways. She was surely the incarnation of particular energies that make the world go round and are worth watching, but not admiring.

Clara's elegance came from her moral strength: she was not one to be pulled into other people's petty dramas, nor was she taken off balance by the imbalance of others. She had her own great interests. She was immensely curious about Russia and was determined to go there to see the bold experiment in human freedom — which is what most of us thought it was — for herself. She insisted that I go with her. I expect she thought we would stop by Constantinople to fetch Trotsky and take him with us. Trotsky was the answer, she insisted, not this Stalin bully.

She found cheap passage: we could go in the summer, working our way across Europe and back, with a month in Moscow to learn everything. It seemed incredible, but why not? We talked about it as we fixed salads and cooked dinners—usually hot dogs or hamburgers, soup or macaroni on the two-burner stove.

"Really, Dottie, there are people traveling all over the world every day. The little hotels and trains are just full of people on adventures. Why shouldn't we be out there, too? Trees have to stay in one place, but we have legs, don't we?"

Jim thought it was crazy talk. He was no booster of the Bolsheviks or any other foreign revolutionaries.

"But what do you think of this Trotsky fellow?" I asked him. "Couldn't he make it all work if he got in power instead of Stalin—don't you think?"

Jim rolled his eyes. Trotsky was exiled in Turkey at the time. Jim had no truck with any of them. He was a free-enterprise New Englander and didn't trust any kind of overly concentrated power, and he was right. Besides, he was set on one more Nantucket summer, then a calm life as an economist or a banker. Why derail all that to go gawk at a bunch of Bolsheviks?

He did not mention my budding acting career as a reason to stay. I therefore realized he did not take it seriously, or take me seriously as a creative person. All the more reason to go gawk at Bolsheviks and have some adventures, I decided. It would make me more interesting.

I was about to write a letter to the two women of Nantucket to tell them I would not be available, when news came from New York City that Clara's parents, who owned a small grocery store there, had been robbed and badly beaten. Crime seemed to be rising everywhere as the Depression deepened, although that was really a mass delusion—crime was going down as people regrouped with their families. Just the same, the beating was real enough, and Clara insisted that her parents lock up the store and just come to Boston to regain their health and their courage—they were both petrified of New York streets now. The King found them a suitable suite nearby, and Clara found herself working as their caregiver. The longer they stayed, the more dependent they became on her, and it was soon clear that Russia was off.

Indeed, dreams were falling like dead leaves around us. Vera was corresponding with a wealthy chap she had dated in high school. Ramona was thinking she might need secretarial school to augment her acting career. Bobbie, however, was steadfast: she even knew the very building on Forty-seventh Street in New York where we could all have an apartment together, in the heart of the theater district.

Jim was frustrated by the fact that even though I now had an apartment away from the glaring stare of the women proctors of Franklin Square House, I was still sticking to my promise to my mother to save sex for marriage. The Lulu thing had reinforced that. Jim was fine with it for the most part, but we necked a lot. He surely needed kisses; he had always just visited another hundred offices with his résumés and calling cards. He was qualified as a geologist or as an economist, but there were no jobs of either kind available. He kept pushing his cart between the bookstore and the train station, his clothes and mood becoming worn.

"You wouldn't know it to look at me," he said one evening, looking down at his worn trousers, "but you and I are going to be rich someday." I completely believed my handsome Phi Beta Kappa.

We were having a little party on Joy Street when he straggled in one night, having visited the state offices just around the corner. My old friends Bobbie, Ramona, and Vera were visiting and drinking.

Jim said he had been at the office of the state's securities department and had actually met the man who turned down Boston Edison for its stock split, which some people took as the first moment of the crash.

"If he still has a job, they should have room for someone like me," he said as Clara handed him a gin fizz with a cherry. She particularly liked cheering him up.

"Do tell," she encouraged his story.

"So I asked him why he did it."

"You didn't! Did you really?" she egged, conducting him with her long cigarette holder. Jim continued:

"He said he was having lunch one day back then at La Seville and a girl cornered him and was very eloquent about how Boston Edison was making life miserable for everyone, and he was moved by her plea to stick up for the people."

"My God," I said. I was transfixed. "All I said was . . ."

"Oh, Dottie, that must have been you!" Vera said, toasting her drink toward me. "You did cause the crash and this damned Depression, didn't you? Well, I guess we love you anyway."

Her glass remained high:

"To our very own Typhoid Mary, our Mrs. O'Leary's cow. Take your pick."

There was a strange silence.

I said something in a small voice:

"I was just trying to . . . All I said was to them was . . ."

But Jim could no longer contain himself. This was all a practical joke, and now Jim laughed, spraying out about half his drink into a gin mist through the apartment. Everyone, except possibly me, thought the whole joke was quite funny. He had indeed been hobnobbing in the state offices, but not that particular office. It was Vera's idea. She could never let that story go. She lightly hugged me, unable to do more on account of her gin and her cigarette. Ramona gave me a better hug and said people were so mean, weren't they?

The trumped-up guilt somehow remained in my mind. Funny how we think we are so special, even in negative ways. It occurred to me that perhaps I was not cut out for a public life in any kind of spotlight. A public life has a lot of responsibility, and you can mess things up for many people if you don't know just what you're doing. I felt the spotlight receding from my life a little in that evening. I just wished Jim would find a good job and he could marry me and take me to bed and I could finally find out what that was all about. That's all I wanted to do that evening, even if he was so mean.

We were necking later in the dark and I whispered into his ear, "I want to be married, and you know why." I took his hand closer to me.

After a long kiss he said, "Emerson would kick you out, you know."

"We'll keep it a secret," I said. Indeed, Emerson and most other schools would not allowed married girls to stay enrolled, as there were usually but a few weeks between marriage and pregnancy in those days — no pills to make it otherwise. And pregnancy was a delicate thing back then, with many women dying in childbirth. Besides, what did a homemaker need with college?

"We'll see," Jim said. I felt him wanting to do this.

Bobbie told me I was crazy. She was the only person I could confide in. She was a dark, private person who just didn't gossip, ever. But she did not like this idea of my marrying Jim.

"I thought you wanted us all to move to New York and get a place and get onto Broadway," she said.

That seemed so impossible. That seemed like something from another world. Were there not soup kitchens now on Broadway?

"Jim's going to get a job with a bank or the government and you'll just be cooking at home and playing bit parts in community theater. And that's just stupid. Jim's a nice boy, but there's no reason for you to sacrifice your life on account of the fact that he's a nice boy." She was pacing around the costume department. She had come to visit me on a Saturday after a play just to set me straight after I had hinted to her backstage that Jim and I might get married. Miss Bailey was not there — this thing could not be said aloud to any staff member — that would be curtains for me. Even Bobbie's shouting at me was in hushed tones, glancing at doorways.

"Stu-pid, stu-pid, stu-pid," she finally said in tears, as if I had just killed someone, which was close to the fact. If I were to turn my back on her and all our plans, she said, surely I was turning my back on my own freedom and a creative life. I sensed the truth of that, and I wept a little with her. But she finally understood that I wanted to do this, and she agreed to be my maid of honor.

■ ■ ■

Trinity Church at Copley Square in Boston is an architectural marvel. The great architect Henry Hobson Richardson designed it, and Boston was still in awe of it, though it was already sixty years old when Jim and I slipped down its great aisle to be married. A minister that Jim knew at Amherst had moved to Boston and performed the marriage. It was a tiny, secretive affair in such a grand space. The minister, the maid of honor, and the best man would be the only people attending.

The minister, who was a bishop, was some time later visiting Emerson, also on Copley Square back then, and he mentioned that he had recently officiated at the marriage of an Emerson student.

I still have no idea why he said it. I am quite sure he was just not thinking. But Emerson went wild with speculation. The administration, its eyes bulging in murderous trance, could not get the name out of the bishop — he realized his slip as soon as he uttered it. But others were interrogated. My circle of friends was well known.

It must have been Bobbie who told them. She denied it in tears, but I could tell — her breakdown was so complete. It is possible she loved me in ways I did not understand — I will never know. But I wish that I had comforted her, as something indeed had broken her heart. Most treachery is but the action of a broken heart.

I was summoned. I was informed that I was to be immediately expelled.

But Emerson teaches you to think carefully and speak effectively. I stood my ground.

"I am responsible for all the costumes for the Emerson Children's Program this spring," I said. "If I leave, it will be nearly impossible for Miss Bailey to train someone in time to do the work properly. She cannot do it alone. So, what I am suggesting is that you let me finish my term. I will leave in the spring, at the end of my junior year. My grades are excellent."

There was then a long stare from the assembled administrators.

"We will let you know this afternoon."

They accepted my offer, but it changed everything, of course. It would mean I could not pursue a serious acting career. Without the degree and their good word, I would be suitable for some chorus line.

We found an apartment just off Joy. Jim and I were finally together. We ate tiny meals and were hungry much of the time. Entertainment took the form of attending Billy Sunday's and Aimee Semple McPherson's traveling big tent revivals, where we marveled at their ability to manipulate people into money-dispensing zombies we hardly recognized as human. The events were free, if you could keep clear of the baskets.

I wanted to go dancing some evenings, but Jim insisted that dancing was "courting business," and that he had danced enough. So I danced alone to the gentle jazz that wafted up Beacon Hill every evening. But it broke my heart for him to say that.

I had less time for my old friends from Emerson, but we did sometimes go down to the Hotel Bradford where WBZ Radio had its studios. Like most Westinghouse stations, it had started out in the 1920s as a nonprofit service to advance education in the community. Most of the programs were created and performed by community volunteers. But as more and more stations went on the air, and as the competition between stations grew, some stations employed professional staffs and produced professionally written and acted dramas, and sold advertisements to pay the higher costs. WBZ had undergone all this, too, but even in the 1930s they sometimes allowed Emerson students to read a part in a radio drama, especially if a paid actor hadn't shown up in time. So we went and hoped for a chance to be on the air — it was great fun.

Gordon Swan, who was the "foley man" who could create absolutely any sound effect for any radio drama, was worth the price of admission — which was free.

At the end of April 1932, the famous, nine-hundred-pound King Leo the Lion arrived at WBZ from Hollywood to promote some MGM movies in public appearances and radio interviews where he would roar on cue. Jim and I were too tired to go, but Bobbie went.

After the program she crashed into Clara's apartment, where Jim and I were visiting, as usual. She was a mess — a wild woman.

"Oh, he was big," she said of Leo the Lion. "God, I'm in love! He looked so fierce, waiting for the show. His real name is Slats, not Leo, and a Mr. Phifer, whom I met, is his trainer and can make him growl or roar as he pleases. Anyway, the poor thing had to wait a long time. Everyone looked unsure of him. When the MGM publicity man brought in the photographers with all the flashes, Leo roared, twisted around, and jumped through the plate glass between the studio and the control room! He just jumped through that thick glass like it was waxed paper!"

We all knew the booth very well, and we knew the men in it. We actresses flirted with them endlessly, hoping they would put us first in line if lightning were to strike.

Bobbie fanned more air to her face so she wouldn't faint. She went on: "Well, those boys went into action, let me tell you! They grabbed their stools and started yelling—the fellow reading the news kept going and mentioned that a famous guest had arrived and was creating quite a stir! So the boys hung together and held up the stools like a big porcupine until Leo jumped back into the studio, which made the news announcer scream on air. Well, there were about a hundred and fifty of us watching from the corridor, through the other huge window, and some were laughing like crazy, including me."

Jim was transfixed. Clara was silently laughing, slapping her legs. She was on the piano stool, bent in half.

"So he settled down, Leo did, I mean Slats, poor Slats, and they went right into the interview a few minutes early. The announcer asks the lion how he likes the pretty girls in Boston, and Mr. Phifer pats him and he makes a nice growl, which was pretty funny. Then the announcer says he has seen MGM films before, but can't be sure this is the same lion until he hears a roar. Could you please prove that you are the real King Leo of MGM fame? So Mr. Phifer grabs and wags some fur on the lion's rump and Slats makes this huge roar. A fantastic roar—I can't believe you weren't listening!

"Anyway, a remaining piece of glass fell out of the booth window with a big crash and spooked him again. He came right at us! He jumped right at us and came right through the window! Right at me!"

Clara had her hand over her mouth. Jim stood up. It was not the kind of story he could listen to sitting down.

"My God!" he said.

"So it was every man for himself!" Bobbie continued. Clara's silent laughs started to find air. She was wailing with mirth.

"So, some go for the elevators and some go for the stairs. I figured, hey, just my luck I'll go into an elevator and Leo, I mean Slats, will come in, too, or into the stairway with me, if I go there. So I just spin around in the lobby and don't know what to do, and Leo is spinning around, roaring, taking swipes in the air, knocking into people with his big head. Everyone was screaming like crazy."

Clara was now on the floor. She was red with it, all but foaming at the mouth.

"So there are three cops now, one of them, and I don't know where he grabbed it, but he actually had a whip, maybe it belonged to Mr. Phifer. The other two cops had chairs. The cop with the whip was fantastic, calm, a master of the moment. The beast could see the cop was the boss, so he backed down the hall, back into the studio, where they put him in his cage. Thank God nobody had a gun, or poor Slats would be dead."

Clara was a heaving mass below the jungle mural. She hadn't had a good laugh in months. She was clawing the rug and whimpering.

"Nobody got hurt?" Jim asked.

"People got knocked around pretty good. The glass cut some people, I think. There was some blood around, but nobody got eaten."

This made Clara snort and curl up in convulsions.

I then noticed Bobbie had a cut on her shoulder. There was a small rip in her blouse and some blood showing around it. I looked at it to make sure there wasn't a piece of glass sticking in her. It was just a scrape. She didn't know that six people had been hurt in the affair, but we would all read about it in the morning paper—nothing too serious.

"Well, my God, Bobbie!" Jim said, handing her a gin. "Are you all right? It must have been an awful scare!"

Bobbie was sitting now. She looked up at him with tears in her eyes.

"I'm fine, honestly. It was beautiful. And, you know? The damn show went on."

Indeed, live radio never cut to something taped, because there was no tape.

Then she started to cry. Clara clomped over on her knees and held her.

"The thing is," Bobbie said, "I'm not afraid of things right now. I mean, the show is always going to go on, isn't it?" She drank her gin and smiled, but she was still weeping, too. She patted Clara, who had kissed her wound and buried her head into Bobbie's tiny chest.

It had been a hard few years for everyone. A month earlier, the little baby of Charles and Anne Lindbergh had been kidnapped in New Jersey, and everybody was sick about it—everybody felt like they were family. And the stock market. And the no jobs. Everything. The baby's body would be found that May. Al Capone had arrived in prison. The 1920s had roared right into the '30s, but now it was clear that all that was over. It was curtains, as we said, taking it from the gangster films.

When the spring ripened, Jim and I packed up for one more summer in Nantucket. We didn't know what we would be doing after that.

At least for the summer, Jim had his lifeguard job again, and I had my position at the Old Parliament House. Ramona had other plans, waitressing, I think.

Leaving Joy Street involved nothing of ceremony, though the King landlord came over and hugged us both, and his eyes were wet. He had a thing for Jim, but he loved me, too.

"Don't give up, Dottie," he said to me tenderly. "You have a great talent, everyone knows that. Don't go be a housewife for this oaf. You got too much sparkle."

I gave him a kiss on his lips, and then surrendered for a long while into his luxurious hug. He was protecting, in that moment, all my dreams for a creative life.

I said good-bye.

here was a stream of people like us leaving Boston, New York, leaving all the big cities, leaving all those communities dedicated to the creative magnification of life, heading home to the dull cold of farms and tiny towns. Jim was lifeguard again and I was maid again on Nantucket—our fourth and final summer there. We walked together in the evenings, but now as man and wife. Jim was allowed to share my room upstairs.

One evening as we walked together I decided I simply must have some potato chips. Jim bought me some from a small food vendor. I ate them, but then I lost them. Jim and I looked at each other. The ladies at Old Parliament confirmed it. They were certain I was pregnant. I was. They were delighted. I didn't know how to feel about it. I was scared for us and for the child. There was some exchange of notes between my mother, Jim's mother Aggie, and me regarding whether or not I should go through with it, considering the present economy and Jim's situation. It was an awful thought. Jim wouldn't hear of it, which was also the way I felt.

The ladies of the Old Parliament used all their local muscle to try to get Jim a job teaching on the island. But the Depression had caused everyone to pull in their jazz hands, and a local boy with lesser credentials got the only available teaching post.

At the end of the summer, we sailed on a ferry among huddled masses returning to what everyone rightly assumed would be hard times on the mainland; we left the privileged class behind, our shallow pockets filled with our summer wages.

We showed up at my parents' house in Laconia. My mother would not have us. I had made my bed and must sleep in it, is precisely what she said. My father seemed crushed by her words, but he did not countermand her. I knew it was the business with Lulu that had so poisoned her attitude toward me. And now, look, I was pregnant, and she would never be the mother of a rich star.

We went to Lakeport, just north of Laconia, to the home of Jim's parents, Aggie and Joe. My Jim didn't need to ask them—he knew it was his house, his family, and he had a right to be there with his new wife. The house would be full, as there were three Haddock children still at home, and now a fourth had come back with a pregnant wife.

"We're going to live here for a while," he told me on the porch as we arrived, hugging me and the baby in me.

So we were now living in an unheated attic. Jim's brother Lawrence, twenty-two, was below us, along with Aggie and Joe, and thirteen-year-old Bradley. A daughter, sixteen-year-old Natalie, would soon leave for teacher's school and let us have her room. But for now it was cold, and the Depression was on. It was the fall of '32 and then the winter of '33. Franklin Delano Roosevelt had just been elected president. We would all listen to his inauguration speech on a small radio in the Haddocks' sitting room. Lawrence, my age, figured himself a Republican and didn't like FDR at all. He also wasn't happy that Jim and I were living there. He was the handsomer son—broad-shouldered, tall, even more athletic than very athletic Jim. Lawrence the football star had led the high school graduation march, voted king by the student body. During my performance as seer and prognosticator on that graduation day, I had publicly teased Lawrence—again at the suggestion of Alan Ayer—about how easily he blushed. So he was dead set against me and would remain so for years. Lawrence was now in his senior year at the University of New Hampshire, which wasn't far away, so he was often in the house, especially on the weekends.

Jim was the educated one, the Amherst intellectual, and he didn't feel he lived in his brother's shadow in any way. My Jim was impressed with FDR, and so was I.

"I will wear whatever color shirt Mr. Roosevelt wants us to wear," Jim said, joking about the frightening rise of authority in Germany. It did seem a time for strong leadership. People are suckers for that in times of trouble.

Just enough heat rose through the house, and there were just enough blankets, and a big fur pelt from a bear or I don't know what, that I could make a morning nest and look out the dormer window at the bare ruined choirs of winter. I imagined my friends still in Boston, starting their senior year and making plans for New York. They, of course, were on their own troubled paths into hard times, and my imaginings about them were really just that. Bobbie would stick it out, though—I was sure of that. I expected Ramona would have to work a few waitress jobs to keep her mother and her siblings fed. I couldn't imagine what Lulu would do, but then perhaps I could—she would do what she had to do to survive, and she was capable of anything. I expected Vera's family would tighten their belts and survive, as the rich have deep resources and connections. There would be fewer dinners at the country club, and they would let one or two of the maids go—toss them overboard. But they would get along. She would be married off to someone with resources. I could prognosticate all that without difficulty. It would whittle down to Bobbie in terms of creative survivors.

Well, she could have Broadway; all I wanted was a potato chip. I saw them in the clouds, in peeling paint, in soiled footsteps in snow. I begged Jim for a potato chip. Such a thing cost a fortune for us now. I felt my growing belly and wondered if the little creature would ever know the heaven of a potato chip. Oh, little baby, there once was a thing, so thin and crispy, so salty and slippery to the tongue—a fragile, blessed host that brought summer and youth to our hearts—and never two alike in all the world! And how they blessed him who gaveth and her who filled up her cheeks with 'em.

The crinkle of a bag of potato chips is a distinctive sound. One attuned to it and to nothing else might hear it coming from a long way away, as a cat hears some faint noise at feeding time. My ears and nose perked as Jim entered the house below. He had squandered a good few pennies of our remaining fortune on a fine sack of lovely Tri-Sum potato chips. He entered smiling. I did not know if I wanted first to make love to him or to eat the chips, so we did both. I hoarded the chips up there for two days, carefully brushing any telling crumbs from my face and sweater before going downstairs.

Aggie and Joe, Jim's parents, were good souls. To earn a few extra dollars, Aggie began teaching English to immigrants in the evenings. By moonlight and starlight, if any, she would climb long, steep Clinton Street all the way home to our house at 32 Prospect.

Joe, who was a machinist at a Scott & Williams factory, also managed horses for people—though most of that business was drifting away.

He was a champion racer of horses, often entering the two-wheeled sulky harness races. He looked like Ben Hur when racing—furiously, dangerously tipping around the curves in a pounding storm of sweat and flying mud. Jim was proud of his father in many ways, but mostly the racing and the fact that Joe had been a champion hockey player in his youth—he was still all muscle and positive thinking. Even so, he didn't win every time.

Jim and his father thought hard about how to keep food on the table and the others in school. Two of Joe's three horse boarding clients had disappeared, or rather their checks had stopped coming, but the horses still had to be fed, and Joe wasn't going to let them starve. The races would bring in some cash, if Joe kept winning, but that was not much money—about enough for the hay.

Joe and Jim came up with a plan for extra cash: the public ice-skating rinks of Laconia and Lakeport were essentially abandoned by the two towns, owing to budget cutbacks. Perhaps we could take them over, clean them up, make them more attractive, and give the towns a bit of profit in the bargain. Joe, being a former hockey star, and Jim, an Amherst man who might be counted on to manage something well, made their pitch to the towns and secured contracts. They were then working day and night to fix up the rinks and prepare them for reopening. I saw very little of my husband in those first weeks, as I could not ice skate in my condition, or be out in the winter days and nights with him. My loneliness, and therefore my personal depression, grew cold and deep. Lawrence had a little job in town, so he was gone most of the time, too. The smaller kids were usually in school or out sledding and skating.

There was a knock on the door one day. It was a friend of Aggie's, Marianna Cogswell. Each autumn, Marianna would get all last year's best-selling books for free from her wealthy friend, Charlotte Kimball, who lived in an actual castle, Kimball Castle, on Locke's Hill, overlooking Lake Winnipesaukee, which defines the region. Mrs. Cogswell, a good friend of Aggie's, was seventy-two and unmarried. She was financially independent—the Cogswells are very old New England—and had taken upon herself to spread good literature around Lakeport, going to her friends' houses with her big basket of books, handing them out to the persons she thought would most enjoy them.

Aggie called me downstairs to meet Mrs. Cogswell and to borrow one of her books. We had a long chat about Emerson and literature. The price of her free library was that when you returned the book to her home, you sat at tea and told her what you thought of it for an hour or more.

"I see," she might say, "so it seems as if Mr. Faulkner is letting Dilsey hold everything together in a very loose but important way. Do you think she realizes she is doing that? Is her love like the dumb love of a dog, or is it very conscious and purposeful, do you think?"

And of course you would have to consider all that and discuss it. There was no reason, as Mrs. Cogswell saw it, why our little hill could not be its own university, since we all were there and had good minds.

Mrs. Cogswell helped me remember who I was. That is often the most important thing we can do for each other, after expressing our love. And she introduced me to my own former English teacher from high school, Edith "Grammy" Swain, who also lived on that hill. Grammy, seventy, also unmarried, lived with her mentally ill mother and with a friend named Fannie Allis, who was sixty-eight and also an educator.

These remarkable women were probably single by choice, but one would not have imagined asking them intimate questions like that. It was certainly the case that many of the men of their generation were missing in action. They were not the dead of the Civil War, but the sons and daughters of that war's survivors. The war so disrupted farms, families, towns, and social life that many sons took off for the West. They fought in the Indian wars, filled mining boom towns, built ranches and new cities, and gradually stopped writing. Many childhood girl-friends were left behind on lonely hilltops.

As I came closer to delivering our child, Jim worried about the coming doctor bill. He found the best family doctor in town, and he asked if there was any trade he might work out. The doctor said he preferred cash, as so many of his patients were no longer paying their bills and he and his wife were hard pressed to put food on their own table. What was of equal concern to the doctor was that these families were not getting medical care, as they were too embarrassed to come in to see him while they owed money. Jim thought about that, and he asked the doctor if he had considered putting everyone on a payment plan, so that at least a little money would be coming in, and people could continue coming in for medical help. The doctor loved the plan. With the doctor's blessing, Jim visited all the patients who were in arrears and signed them up. For a few dollars a month, which Jim would go around and collect, the patients in fact regained their pride and were soon back in his waiting room. And Jim had earned a baby delivery for me.

That somehow did not make the delivery easier. I went into the hospital once and was sent home. Finally, baby Elizabeth was born. She was beautiful. Mean brother Lawrence was head over heels for the little thing, though he tried not to show it at first. But the baby was a great joy to an otherwise glum household. Everything was beautiful now. Little knitted presents came from everywhere. Even my own mother, such a stick-in-the-mud about my leaving school and marrying, was a new person now. The work for me was considerable. Making enough hot water to clean the diapers was a day in itself. Everything took forever, and I was nursing and not getting much sleep.

As spring arrived, the ice rinks closed down. Joe and Aggie and the two smaller children packed up to follow the spring and summer races. Jim continued to work for the doctor and continued sending out his résumé. He was gone much of the time in town.

Finally alone with Elizabeth that first morning after Joe and Aggie left, I went downstairs to fix some dinner and warm up the house, and I realized that Aggie had not left any firewood for me. She normally ordered it from a woodsman who delivered it. She had not done so. I was angry with her for not caring. With little "Betty" on my back, I went out in the melting snow and into the woods to find broken branches and bring them in, dragging them in one by one. I broke off what I could with my bare hands. I was crying as I gathered the wood and broke it up, but I got it done. When I was cooking, finally, and finally warm, I realized what had happened: Aggie was forced to decide between buying wood and buying gasoline to follow the races. She couldn't stand the idea of telling me that we were too broke for a wood delivery, so she decided to let me think she had just forgotten about it. She knew I could find enough wood to get by, but she just couldn't have that conversation. And she couldn't gather it herself without Joe seeing her and delaying the trip and missing the first races, which paid good money to the winners. I cried again, this time for her and not for me. But all I ever really had to do to cheer up was to look at my baby.

The ladies of the hill, too, were enchanted by little Elizabeth, who was very bright from the start. Now that I was a mother with great responsibilities, Aggie and Grammy Swain and Marianna decided to think creatively for me.

Grammy Swain, I should mention, was sometimes the object of ridicule when I was in high school, because she nearly always wore the same, slightly tattered black dress and seemed hopelessly old-fashioned. She was, in fact, a suffragette who had worked hard for the women's vote and was still very active in that continuing work. The kids may have made fun of her, but she didn't care about that because she was so busy caring about them. I remembered her as a kind and serious teacher. She liked the fact that I could easily memorize and beautifully recite the long poems she assigned, and of course we cannot help but like the people who think we are special. It was she, of course, who drilled Shakespeare into us, including Portia's speeches from *The Merchant of Venice*. For that I owed her my admission to Emerson, at least.

Her house looked haunted. She allowed almost no visitors inside, as her mother was quite mentally ill and was kept in an enclosure of some kind in the kitchen. I hesitate to use the word cage, but I suppose that is what it was. Aggie had been inside the house once and had seen it.

Grammy Swain was happy to receive visitors on her porch, how-ever, and she sent for me one afternoon and sat me down on the di-lapidated porch for tea and cookies. Soon, Mrs. Cogswell arrived.

"Doris, dear, we have been thinking about you," Grammy Swain began.

They both attended monthly luncheons of the League of Women Voters. Grammy was the county chairwoman.

"We conduct business, then have the lunch, then we visit," Mrs. Cogswell described. I thought I was going to be asked to join.

"Yes," Grammy took over, "and we were thinking that the meet-ings would be much more fun and we could get attendance higher if we provided a little entertainment."

"So what would you say, Doris," said Mrs. Cogswell, "if the League hired you for, say, twenty-five dollars, to provide a one-woman play during the lunch portion? We were thinking of J. M. Barrie's little one-act play, *The Twelve Pound Look*. You could play all the parts, couldn't you? You have such a memory for lines."

In fact I loved that play. Twenty-five dollars was a fortune—five hundred bags of potato chips.

"And if it works out," Mrs. Cogswell continued, "then we can do it again, for another fee, of course. And there are other League meetings in the surrounding counties, if the idea is well received. It would be up to you to put on a good show and get people talking, League to League."

I should mention that *The Twelve Pound Look*, though written by a man (Barrie wrote *Peter Pan*, of course), was about the arrival in culture of the working woman. The star is a woman who is sent by a stenography service to type a letter for the rich man to whom she had once been married. In the process, she encounters the new wife, who is the woman she might have become. Years earlier, rather than continue to serve in the great man's generous but dehumanizing shadow, she had purchased an old typewriter for twelve pounds and left him for a modest career. It foreshadowed my own domestic situation in the years ahead, of course, and that of so many husbands and wives in a changing America. It was the perfect play for the ladies of the League of Women Voters to enjoy after lunch.

> KATE. [*Blithely.*] It is work I have had some experience of. [*She proceeds to type.*]
>
> LADY SIMS. But you can't begin till you know what he wants to say.
>
> KATE. Only a specimen letter. Won't it be the usual thing?
>
> LADY SIMS. [*To whom this is a new idea.*] Is there a usual thing?
>
> KATE. Oh, yes. [*She continues to type, and Lady Sims, half-mesmerized, gazes at her nimble fingers. The useless woman watches the useful one, and she sighs, she could not tell why.*]
>
> LADY SIMS. How quickly you do it! It must be delightful to be able to do something, and to do it well.
>
> KATE. [*Thankfully.*] Yes, it is delightful.
>
> LADY SIMS. [*Again remembering the source of all her greatness.*] But, excuse me, I don't think that will be any use. My husband

wants me to explain to you that his is an exceptional case. He did not try to get this honor in any way. It was a complete surprise to him.

KATE. [*Who is a practical Kate and no dealer in sarcasm.*] That is what I have written.

LADY SIMS. [*In whom sarcasm would meet a dead wall.*] But how could you know?

KATE. I only guessed.

Each change of character required a shift of stance and of voice. This was very comic in itself. All the stage directions from Mr. Barrie were a joyful aid.

Later in the play, Kate says: "If I was a husband—and it is my advice to all of them—I would often watch my wife quietly to see whether the twelve-pound look was not coming into her eyes." And at the very end, the man's newer wife asks how much a typewriter might cost.

Well, it was not Broadway, but the women would be a good audience, and I would be adding to the family income—and having a creative outlet at the same time. So of course I said yes. I was jumping inside.

Aggie made me an elegant blouse that worked easily for nursing Elizabeth. For the first performance at the first League meeting, Jim waited outside in the rattletrap old car he had bought to get to the skating rinks and odd jobs. He held and rocked Elizabeth out in the cold—she was well wrapped—and I would duck out from time to time to feed her.

I was embarrassed toward the end of the play when I looked down and saw my front was all wet—I was leaking. I apologized, but most of the ladies in the audience had been there themselves and said so. I continued to the big finish.

The bookings for my one-woman shows grew gently. With the rink money, Joe's race winnings, Aggie's teaching money, my performance money, and with a remarkable amount of stretching of food and fuel and patched clothes, we were getting by.

■ ■ ■

"My God, Dottie!"

It was Lulu at the open front door, looking over my short self to the house beyond. We had corresponded a few times, but not about her coming. She had taken the morning train up from Boston and would return on the evening train. I could see she was appalled by our modest circumstances. Aggie was embarrassed by the home.

"It's so good to see you," Lulu said as she hugged me. She was in her flapper best, while I felt homespun, dowdy and poor.

We walked in the snow, and she told me what she was up to, which was mostly waitress work and finishing up at Emerson. She said Boston was not the same without me, as there was no one to care about her anymore, or to get angry with her for being such a bother. I told her about my little one-woman, one-act performances. She laughed.

"No, darling, I'm sorry. It's wonderful. I was laughing at you for another reason, really. I had the impression that your in-laws' house was very grand. I'm sure it was just something I expected and that perhaps you didn't bother to correct. It's very nice, of course."

We turned and looked at the house, and I laughed. So did she. I had little Elizabeth bundled against me, and I just sat down in the snow, as did Lulu, and we laughed and couldn't stop laughing.

"I'm sorry you came on the help's day off," I said in Emerson English. I was suddenly homesick for Emerson and Boston and especially Joy Street.

"So?" she said into a silence. "Lawrence? And how is he?"

Ah, I suddenly understood.

Lawrence had visited our Joy Street jungle once with his brother, my Jim. He had come back a second time with some of his fraternity brothers from the University of New Hampshire. Our little apartment was, to such boys, the essence of bohemian fun. It was very tame, of course, compared with the life of artists only a few doors away, but it was hot stuff for country boys.

When Lawrence had visited, his varsity physique and handsome face had been noticed most carefully by Lulu, who was at the apartment often after our reconciliation. He had the swagger of a rich boy, and she assumed he was.

In fact Lawrence was in love, desperately so, with the beautiful daughter of one of Laconia's wealthiest families. She was an expert horsewoman, which made Lawrence adore her all the more. Her life was the fantasy he wanted: beautiful wife, stable of fine horses, something of a grand house and horse farm. It was not to be. She would throw him over for a rich boy more suitable to her country club set.

He was still in shock from this. Lulu, who was an easy lay, could have swept him away for a time of special comfort, and then trapped him forever. But would she really, now that she had seen the family house? I sensed that she was interested anyway—Lawrence looked like a man who would go places, Depression or not, which is exactly what I still thought about Jim.

"So where is he?"

His cool cruelty toward me was something that came into my mind. I knew my next words could be important. Should I tell her he was available for collection from the curb? Would I not tell him that she had used a pregnancy to falsely shake down an innocent rich boy? The potential for an interesting pairing was indeed the stuff of a good drama, and a drama student appreciates such things. I could easily ask Lulu to spend the night and take the morning train instead. I knew Lawrence was expected at dinner or soon after, and a match could be made that evening.

In hard economic times, you can't help but think about guarding your limited resources. The Haddock house was crowded. I may have worried, even slightly, about what would happen to Jim and Betty and me if Lawrence suddenly took a wife. I worried about what my mother would think of me if I were still associated with Lulu.

"He's away at school," I finally said. It was the truth, but hardly honest.

"Oh. Well, damn it, Dottie, I need a good guy right now. Lawrence is like a god, don't you think? I've written him, hinting that he should invite me up, but he never writes back. Don't tell him I came. Maybe I'll come back some other time. You can maybe let me know when he will be here?"

"Sure," I lied. I decided I would spare him his Lulu year. Even so, I understood that I loved her as a friend. She was trouble and something to be kept far from fragile friends and family, but there was something about her vitality. She was the life force itself—imperfect, sadly tragic, dangerous, but undeniably interesting—an attractive nuisance. I walked her to the station, stopping on the long way home to nurse Elizabeth in the woods. In that suckling moment I was sad for the life I had abandoned in Boston, and yet, looking down at my sweet Elizabeth, who needed me so, I was happy for this new life. It was an impossible mix of emotions. The trees towered and swayed above me—above us.

THE MAIN COURSE OF LIFE

10

*I*n the days to come, Jim would receive a letter from his old professor, who had just then been appointed to a considerable position in the new Roosevelt administration. It was a clear invitation to come to Washington so that the professor might introduce him around. Jim almost did not show me the letter. When he did, and when I asked why he was not excited, he choked up a little as he explained:

"I have nothing to wear, Dottie, nothing." His good clothes had been ruined during his hard work pushing the book carts around Boston. He now had old farm clothes, which were good enough for his work with the doctor and around the horses and the skating rinks, but not for the marble offices of Washington, D.C.

"Can you imagine how embarrassed old Thorp would be if I showed up like this? It would humiliate him, and me." He sat on the bed and fell back to look up at the roof planks above us.

It seemed like a trivial problem to me—it seemed he was looking for an excuse to not make the big move that he had surely earned and that we needed. If all he required was a new suit to open the door to a new life for us, well, I just didn't think such a thing should be the deciding factor. I knew our own reserves were quite slim. A decent suit in 1933 cost about twenty-five dollars, with another four dollars for dress shoes and maybe that much again for a decent hat, which was expected. For under thirty-five dollars, then, plus thirty-eight dollars for the round-trip train ticket to Washington, and three or four dollars per night for a hotel, we should be on our way up. I could pack sandwiches for him and save him meal costs.

"Impossible," he said. "Add it all up!"

He had talked to his mother. She reminded him that the Haddocks were not in the habit of borrowing money, and that the household certainly didn't have that much to spare. Every dollar expected was accounted for, and would provide a family meal or something just as vital. This trip would be a good hundred dollars, she had calculated.

She suggested he have the professor write again if there was a job certain. Then he could go with a one-way ticket, and send for Elizabeth and me when he had his first check in hand.

"I can't write him and say that," Jim said. "Besides, I don't know if we're right for Washington. That's a big rat race there. I don't know if you would like it, either, and now we have the baby."

He was falling, and I couldn't seem to catch him.

"I think I have a chance with the electric company here."

All his door-to-door collecting for the doctor had put him in regular contact with a meter reader who said he might help Jim get a job like that. I couldn't believe it. He was a fallen man, beaten by fear itself. I did not have a strong enough net to save him. The letter from Professor Thorp went unanswered, which was so unlike Jim.

The fact is, an economic depression is an illness that becomes a personal depression. It becomes difficult to see a happy outcome, and so people give up.

I'm not saying Jim gave up. He gave up on his original dreams, but not on life. But, in these little ways, a dollar at a time, we fell into a very modest life, and the days became years.

Jim did, in fact, get a job reading meters. The electric utility transferred him to Nashua, near New Hampshire's border with Massachusetts. Our son, Jim Jr., was born there. We lived in one unit of a building that had been a nursing home of some kind. I talked the owner into letting me use the fallow courtyard for a very large vegetable garden, which soon fed several of the families who lived there and kept a large common room stocked with hundreds of sealed jars of food for all seasons.

We made friends and began to ski together with other couples. Very regularly, Jim visited a pretty young woman to talk politics and other things that perhaps I wasn't as passionate about. He had met her on his meter-reading rounds and told me all about her. I tried not to mind, thinking my relationship with him was secure and that men need their friends as desperately as women need their securities. I was right. I am not suggesting that husbands and wives should give their mates anything less than the full value of their emotional bond, for it is in that promised generosity that we save each other from the loneliness of our mortal situation. But among the useful mysteries of life is the mothlike attraction of men to the fair light of the feminine, and I simply gave him always the benefit of the doubt and was always proved wise to do so. He loved me best and longest.

I never needed to forgive him some great treachery, but I would have. After all, we live in a many-layered world, and we are many-layered people. If one layer of someone's personality flares up and causes us harm, we must try to put it in perspective among all the other layers of that life. A long marriage sometimes requires our willingness to do that.

That view can also help us forgive ourselves our many failings; we are far more than our worst parts.

I loved Jim's creativity: he refused to let a little thing like a Great Depression dampen his spirit for long. He brought home old newspapers, first for us to read so we would be up on everything, then to soak and roll into tight logs to help heat our home.

I became rather good at making one chicken extend nearly all week, as it moved from Sunday dinner to Thursday soup. We mended things. Thin-cut strips of old, ripped clothing became hooked rugs—yarn was too expensive. We spent no dollar we didn't have to. It went on like that through the Depression, and even through the war. I am still like that.

For our daughter, Betty, I started a club for girls so she and her friends would have good activities. One of the girls would later write *Peyton Place*, which, as an account of those times in those towns, was not a surprising story to me or to others I knew. People's creative urges were boiling inside them, and sometimes they were not to be contained.

Ordinary living, common decency, honest relations were the daily norm, of course, and each year of our marriage brought a more solid kind of happiness.

On a long summer hike, Jim and the kids and I met a wealthy couple, Elizabeth and Max, who would become our best friends. We took weekends on their land and in their sugarhouse cabins, always hiking and visiting and putting on little plays on the stage Max built for us all. We wrote our own plays and had a marvelous time.

Max, whose elegant gravity reminded me of Robert Peabody in many ways, had a lovely assistant who was helping him write a book about Shakespeare's *Hamlet* — it became, after his death, an important book for Shakespeare scholars. Elizabeth did not mind when Max and his assistant took long walks to talk about the book. I did not mind when Elizabeth took long horse rides with my Jim. I would usually stay at the main house and read or garden until they got back, and there was never the slightest thought that anyone would ever do anything hurtful, which I trust they did not.

Max saw potentials in me that Alan Ayer had once seen. He encouraged me and mentored me in my career in the shoe manufacturing business. When my children were old enough, I had taken a secretarial job at the Beebee Shoe factory in Manchester, where we were then living. The factory was in one of the old mill buildings along the river. Many of the mills closed down during the Depression and never recovered. Mills sprang up in the South later, where labor was cheaper and snow and ice never barred the way. Then it all went overseas, of course, because the people who had the jobs had no representation in Congress or the White House, and the mill owners did, which all continues today. As for the abandoned buildings along the river, the town of Manchester took them over and rented them out to companies like Beebee in an effort to remake the economic base, which worked to a degree. You can still get pretty good rents there.

In my twenty years at the shoe factory I became, with Max's advice and Jim's encouragement, one of the two highest-paid women in the state. That wasn't saying much, but it was something. As I walked each morning into that huge building, and into the great room where I supervised thirty clerks, I did of course think of how my life's direction had changed, and how I was not walking into some exciting Broadway theater but an old factory. I nevertheless dressed well and I moved well and I used my Emerson voice to command authority and get things done. We became one of the top ten shoe companies in America, back when most shoes were made here. (Many good shoes are still made here, and it's easy to find them, of course, now that we have the Internet.)

Working mothers were not uncommon during the Depression, but it was certainly less common than today. I felt guilty about it, but our children turned out fine. They had summer adventures together at sea and in the woods. My son became a great social service hero — he created new and very humane ways to care for developmentally disabled children and adults in community and family settings, and he worked politically and legally to close down the abusive state institution where such people had been warehoused before. What he did in New Hampshire spread all over America, freeing hundreds of thousands of people to live decent lives, and sparing many families the horror of sending their loved ones away to "cuckoo's nest" institutions when their only "crime" was being a little different, and often different in lovely ways. It took great courage to do all that, because he knew it would come at great cost to himself, which it did. You cannot change big things without suffering for it. The bureaucracies of the status quo are unforgiving of any real improvement. My daughter was no less than my son, and she became a noted psychologist in Washington, D.C.

In midlife, in connection with our church, my husband and I went to Alaska to help stop the testing of hydrogen bombs there. We made lifelong friends of the Inuit people of Point Hope, Alaska, whose community had been at risk. During that time, though my husband led the way, I became more politically active and even became comfortable with asking members of Congress to listen and help, which they did. I also became something of an artist at hooking rugs, many of which I sold to support Native Americans in Arizona who were resisting the strip mining of their lands by Peabody Coal.

My husband constantly explored New England as an amateur geologist, often with our children beside him as his loyal assistants. They lugged great boxes of rocks home from wherever they went.

Though he started out reading meters, Jim became one of the top men at the electric company, always studying more about engineering, electricity, hydropower, and finances. He developed the idea that utility companies could share their extra seasonal capacity, which became the New England grid and eventually the national electrical grid. I'm sure other people were involved too, but as far as the kids and I were concerned, he figured it out all by himself.

We spent as many weekends as possible with our friends Max and Elizabeth. We hiked the mountains above their old sugar farm and enjoyed life. Max and Elizabeth were an education for us: an education in science and nature, and in the kindness of good manners.

I must give you an example: Max was sitting at the great farm's dining table one Saturday night. Into the room ran two students who had been staying in his spare cabin down by the river. They had suffered some difficulty with the fireplace. In fact, they had burned down the cabin, which they announced in tears. We were all shocked, except Max.

Max hardly stopped eating. He motioned for them to get a plate.

"That's wonderful," he said. "We have wanted to build something special down there on the river, and this will give us a chance to do that without feeling guilty about getting rid of that old cabin. It had no good windows for the view. I'll get a crew down there tomorrow to lay it out. Now eat, and we'll get you some bunks up here. No need for this to ruin your weekend."

It was not just that Max was a gentleman, which you can see, but he knew how to roll with life and always make something better of it.

When Jim ate a bad mushroom one weekend and got awfully ill, Max took that as an invitation for us all to learn more about mushrooms. The one Jim ate looked like a harmless variety but turned out to be a dangerous and hallucinogenic laughing gym (*Gymnopilus junonius*). Max ordered two big boxes of books about mushrooms. He became quite an expert, as did all of us, though Max also became a noted scholar on the subject and Elizabeth became an expert on ferns, which she taught me about and which, ever after, made my walks through the woods more meaningful.

My son and daughter picked up on all that, too. Years later Betty, when she was a psychologist living in Washington, D.C., heard about a deadly mushroom growing in the area that looked almost identical to a tasty mushroom that grows in Poland and which every year young Polish girls working in the Polish Embassy in Washington would be tempted to pick. One girl had died. Betty quickly organized an association to reach these young visitors with good information. The organization became an addition to her life, and even now the association prospers and continues its work.

My son, Jim, is one of the best mushroom experts in New Hampshire. It has led him to a wonderful friendship with a Japanese chef in the area. They have helped each other through rough times, including the death of the chef's remarkable wife. I suppose the grace of their friendship came from that moment long ago when Jim's father had a stomachache and Max made something of it.

I have taken those as great lessons: that even the smallest kindness or positive action has great power within it, and that we must turn bad news into good whenever we are able, which is most of the time. It is not just a matter of making repairs when damage happens; it is a matter of creating beautiful things from the broken pieces, and tricking all our pain, even when it seems fathomless, into beauty.

■ ■ ■

Jim and I retired and moved to a new home in the woods of Dublin, New Hampshire, home of the Old Farmer's Almanac, and just up the hill from Peterborough, which is as charming a town as New England provides. Peterborough, as its residents will not tell you because they are sick of hearing it, was the model for *Our Town*, as Thornton Wilder wrote the play there. He wrote it at the MacDowell Colony, which still prospers as an artists' retreat in the woods above town.

After beautiful years in retirement, Jim, my hero husband, contracted Alzheimer's disease. I cared for him for ten years, and then he died.

Max and then his wife, Elizabeth, my best friend, died.

I was quite depressed.

And then there was a whisper in my ear: My son, Jim, was driving me down to visit my sister in Florida. Along the road was an old traveling man, out in the middle of nowhere, just standing there with his knapsack. In an instant, he was far behind us.

The old fellow somehow inspired me. I saw that there was still a great deal of work and joy for me. I decided in that moment to walk across the United States on behalf of my favorite issue, the political reform of our expensive elections. I had been working on that for some time with a group of friends led by Bonnie Riley. I would use the publicity to get people to contact their members of Congress, and we would get a bill passed. Why should I care if it might kill me?

Once I made the decision to walk, every door opened to me. Whenever I needed a special kind of person for the work ahead, someone appeared like magic. Then, on the road, when I needed a place to stay, there it was; when it rained too hard, there was some earthly angel with a great, plastic tarp to walk with me. When the snow was too deep for walking, my old skis showed up and I skied the last ninety or so miles into Washington, along the old C&O Canal, which was surveyed by young George Washington just as though he had done it for me.

You must never doubt that you will be given what you need, once you accept the idea of who you are and what you must do. It is never, ever, ever too late to decide what that is and what you will do about it. I was nearly ninety when I decided.

The walk forced me to do what we all need to do anyway, which is to keep moving. The energy for living a better life requires that you get your ship in shape. You can't just keep it freshly painted; you have to keep it as sleek as you can, and clean your hull of barnacles—those little bits of unfinished business, guilt, and grudges that slow you down. A morning walk is ideal. I'm not suggesting that you walk across the nation, but I am suggesting that a two- or three-mile walk probably won't kill you. And if it does, maybe it's time.

You may have your own idea about getting in shape, but walking is as simple as pie, lets you practice noticing the things of the world, and occasionally sends you home with a new friend. The energy you gain from getting back into shape cannot be overestimated. When I began my long walk, my arthritis and emphysema and bad back were in such a state that some of my grandchildren wagered I would be good for only a few days. But every mile—and then every ten and hundred and thousand miles—improved my health immensely. I got a checkup when I finally reached Washington, D.C.—starting from Los Angeles—and my doctor determined I was physically about ten years younger than when I started.

Since then, I know that when my health goes into a slide, it is because I am not walking enough, so I get outside and find a good cause to walk for or get reacquainted with the villages beyond my woods. Out there on the road, you feel your younger self reemerging and looking around. You will come home physically tired, perhaps, but full of emotional energy and optimism for the day. And you have a very good excuse for a snack and a nap.

You can join a health club and walk on a treadmill, of course, if you enjoy such routines. Better, I think, to see some territory and hazard some risks and adventures. Treadmills are good when the weather is impossible, assuming you cannot ski or skate. I have cut a small cross-country ski trail through my woods and try to use it from time to time when the roads are too snowy for hiking. Now that I am one hundred, I mostly just walk. I think this routine is more important than ever. It won't keep me alive forever, or even much longer, but it will keep me healthy until I die.

I also believe that keeping your personal possessions pared down to the minimum helps you stay active and healthy. If you overload a boat, it can't sail very well. If you can't stand the idea of letting loose of things entirely, wrap them up as presents to your relatives and keep them in the family that way—let the other family boats carry the load.

I saw a fellow interviewed on television once who had just lost his house to a wildfire in the West. The reporter asked him the usual question: "How do you feel, having just lost everything?" The fellow did not give the standard reply. He paused a few seconds, then, maybe not quite believing it himself, said, "You know, I feel good, like all that stuff was weighing me down. I feel a lot lighter now. It feels great, to tell you the truth. Really fine." The reporter went quickly on to find a better victim to interview.

We have been quite thoroughly conditioned to need things around us. Shopping is sometimes our solace and joy. Comfort can come to mean being surrounded by things, things, things. I know people who live very sparely and happily, even though they have the means to buy lots of fine things. But such people are rare today. Of course some of our possessions are precious photos and letters and small mementos that do help us remember who we are. We'll keep those.

For the rest, well, we never own things so much as they own us. They order us about, having us dust them and clean them, repair them, worry after them when we are away, pay for space for them, protect and insure them—the list goes on. The rich, poor dears, have it the worst. They spend half their time worrying about their jewelry and couture clothing and cars and time-share jets. It is tragic. We did an intervention some years ago with a progressive income tax to free them of these burdens, but that has come undone and needs fixing.

■ ■ ■

After I reached Washington, by the way, it took another two years of organizing meetings, rallies, vigils, protests, jail time, fasts, walks, and speeches to get the bill passed. It did pass, making it illegal for corporations to write checks to federal political campaigns. It was later undercut by a Supreme Court decision, but democracy is a running game: you huddle and go back in. You keep going.

In the years after the long walk, I settled back into life in my woods of southern New Hampshire. I sent out several thousand thank-you letters to everyone who had helped me along my way.

It was a time to get to know my grandchildren and great-grandchildren better, and to visit my daughter, who had contracted Alzheimer's disease and would soon die.

My son has been my strength these years. He is stocky, gray-bearded, knit-capped. He is a consummate storyteller. Now retired, Jim is well known in every general store and garage in southern New Hampshire, especially among those men and women most able to defend themselves and return blows in the never-ending double entendre battles that pass for good-humored conversation in the Granite State. The bantering is but a red flannel cover to hide a shy but extravagant neighborly love.

In the winter of 2003 Jim had been boiling down maple syrup near his creek in deep snow when a young deer jumped right over him, slipped on the icy bank of our creek, broke through the ice, fell into the water a bit, then stumbled on, only to be chased by Jim's dogs. Jim ran through impossible snow to stop the attack. The scene moved across the creek and across the road. Jim finally got hold of the dogs, flagged down the brand new and expensive car of a passing neighbor, stuffed his dogs in her back seat — to her horror, as they were bloody — then went on to see that the deer was all right. Jim finally slipped and fell exhausted on a snowy bank, and the young deer stopped running and came to him. Jim stood, and the deer came right up to him, stood on its rear hooves, and pressed its chest against Jim's. Jim laid the deer down in the snow and patted it. He laid himself down next to it. The wild heart of the deer settled as Jim talked to it. After a time, it got up and walked calmly away into the woods. That is who Jim is. And the deer was a sign that life was not finished with any of us just yet.

Soon after that encounter, Jim patted me on my shoulder and said, "You're not through, are you, Ma?" He could see I was restless to be out there somewhere doing something worth my feed. I was ninety-three, but I felt fifteen sometimes.

Some friends had come to see me and to encourage a new adventure. Time and again young spirits will be sent to fetch us, however late, to the great opportunities, the adventures, main battles and mortal risks we were made for. Who are we to merit such attention and persistent invitation? We are more than we can imagine.

11

BACK TO HARVARD

I was on my deck, which extends from my kitchen out into the woods. There is a stream below that makes a lovely sound. It was evening, and I was with my new friends, collected on my long walk. In many ways, they represented—as if there are archetypes at work, I suppose—my college friends from Boston. Molly Ivins was perhaps the new Vera; Blue Broxton the new Bobbie; Dennis and Jim the new Alan Ayer; Bonnie Riley the new Mrs. Southwick; and so on. Our lives do have quite solid patterns, and we attract the same energies over and over again, for good and ill.

"Doris, you go give 'em hell," Molly Ivins said after a few whiskies. It was a summer evening, 2003. Molly, Ronnie Dugger, Betsy Moon, Dennis Burke, Bonnie Riley, Jim Hightower, and my son, Jim, were looking out at the darkening woods and talking about the 2004 election, still more than a year away. Everyone agreed that we all needed to work hard if the country was going to change direction, which we thought was vital. Another debacle like 2000, and the years since, would be too much for the country, we thought.

Dennis, a political organizer who had helped me cross the deserts, had some new figures showing that working women were dramatically underrepresented in voter registration roles. When they did register, they tended to vote progressive.

So it seemed obvious to me what I should do: I should go on the road and help working women get registered to vote, and there was no time to waste.

I was unsure; maybe it would be silly for me to try. I had barely made it home from the last big adventure, and I was older now—ninety-three. Molly winked at me, which meant what the hell. She was wearing a wig at the time, as her breast cancer treatment was well under way. She was in a mood to think that people should do what they want to do while they still could. She had just got some news that day, and she knew that I would outlive her, which I did.

"You go out there—you'll regret it if you don't," she said to me in a big hug.

An idea percolated through the evening: I would not walk across the country, but I would take the old bus—a small motor home—that my friend Ken Hechler, former congressman and West Virginia secretary of state, had donated as a support vehicle for my big walk and which had been moldering ever since under the leaves. I would walk within cities, but not between them, and I would do different kinds of events. Mainly I would take over the jobs of working women long enough for them to go register to vote. We would try to get local television stations and newspapers to cover me doing zany jobs so that women could go register, hoping that the stories would encourage more women to do so. That was the plan. I could perhaps boost the efforts of each city's local voter drives, getting them a little extra publicity and more volunteers.

The vehicle, a bit over the hill, was cleaned up and rechristened Rocinante, pronounced "rose-sin-NAN-tee," which was the name of Don Quixote's faithful steed and also the name of John Steinbeck's camper truck for his *Travels with Charley* adventure. The name would soon be shortened to Rosie, which was especially appropriate when, later in the trip, artists in Asheville painted Rosie the Riveter across her port side. Jim had a mechanic friend give the engine the once-over. It had a chronic overheating problem that we would just have to live with. We couldn't afford a new engine.

Jim and Dennis said they would come with me at least for the first few weeks. They would recruit volunteers along the way to drive me farther and to do advance work. Dennis would provide publicity support and help me with local information for speeches, as he had done on my long walk. Jim would do logistical planning. A progressive support group, Working Assets, gave us a small grant to get started. The rest would have to be donations from our email list, which had grown to twenty thousand or so during my walk across the country.

Regarding the vehicle's interior more generally, it had, as such camper vehicles do, fake wood lamination and upholstered headers that were soon covered with political buttons and stickers; a little dinette stacked with laptop computers and maps; a bench couch; a small kitchen; a tiny bathroom; an overhead sleeping loft for me. Climbing up and down from it was difficult, but good exercise—though whenever possible, which was most of the time, I stayed in the homes of volunteers along the way.

A golden-threaded Gypsy damask hung across the loft for privacy. It reminded me of Ramona. The shower didn't work, but we learned to shower with a one-gallon jug of water, heated with a pint from the teakettle. I had learned to take one-gallon showers when walking across the country, as had Dennis, Jim, Nick Polumbo, John Anthony, Matt Keller, and my many other heroes and latter-day guardian angels.

In early autumn we began. I made a launch speech at Harvard's Kennedy School of Government.

The speaker before me was Lech Wałesa, the Polish president and hero of democracy.

In describing the critical days of the Solidarity movement at the Gdańsk shipyards, he said, "There are special places where you can feel the future." That's how we felt; everyone we knew was organizing to make the coming election mean something. When it was my evening to speak, the Harvard students, layered on balconies around me, gave a cheering ovation to send me on my way.

As I was walking out, a young reporter from the *Harvard Crimson* lightly grilled me:

CRIMSON: When did you start becoming politically active and what inspired you?

DORIS: In 1960 I became active in an effort to save an Eskimo village from being destroyed by hydrogen bomb tests. Dr. Ed Teller, who died last month, wanted to demonstrate that H-bombs could be used to "terraform" harbors and canals. They were having a hard time negotiating with Panama for the canal, and wanted to blast a new one through Nicaragua, and test it first in Alaska, which would have destroyed a fishing village and the livelihood of many people. We organized contact with the House and Senate and slowed it down. When Kennedy signed the atmospheric test ban treaty with Khrushchev, that killed it. I was inspired to get involved in that effort by a minister from that village who was visiting New England. He took us back with him to meet the villagers, and after that we were very involved. It's in my book.

CRIMSON: You are walking across the country to register working women to vote. Where did that idea come from?

DORIS: I'm not walking all the way this time. Last time I walked 3,200 miles, but it took me 14 months. This time I've got 13 months before the election and have 30,000 miles to cover. But even though I'm not walking all that way, traveling isn't easy at my age. But I find that, if you make a real effort, people give you the time of day and will listen to your message. Political leadership, even at my modest level, is about sacrifice. That's what Gandhi taught us, and King.

CRIMSON: Are you actually a grandmother or is "Granny" just an honorific?

DORIS: I am a grandmother and 16 times a great-grandmother.

CRIMSON: During your last protest you were arrested for reading The Declaration of Independence in the Capitol building. Judge Hamilton threw out the case and gave you a hug. Your description makes the reader think you found him kinda cute.

DORIS: He is a tall and dignified African-American man who looks like an actor you would cast for the part of a Washington, D.C., judge. He almost looks too much like a judge. After he complimented us for our brave action and let us out of jail, I thought he looked very wise. I was later arrested for another action in the Capitol, where we were reading the Bill of Rights, and I certainly asked for Judge Hamilton, but they don't do it that way.

CRIMSON: Did Forrest Gump's run across the country influence your protest style?

DORIS: I admit that I looked a little clueless at times, and I am known for eating chocolate. But before you dismiss me entirely, understand that I met with many newspapers along my path, many of which thereafter changed their tune to support the passage of campaign finance reform—including majors like the Dallas Morning News. Also, in the last miles, several thousand people were walking with me into Washington, including several dozen members of Congress, and we had lots of Good Morning America, the Today Show and NPR stories to raise the profile of the reform bill as it hit Congress. Gump had none of that. None of it.

CRIMSON: What has been the funniest or most interesting experience you have had on your walks?

DORIS: Funniest—you can't tell those stories without embarrassing someone (usually me). Most interesting: probably when we were picketing the U.S. House and Majority Leader Gephardt invited a few of us up to his office to warm up. The bill was finally to pass Congress that night, he informed us. He said some nice things about my effort. I said I was but a pinprick. He said, well, we are all just pinpricks. My friend, Dennis, said, well, Congressman, you are at least half-right.

Leaving Harvard, I asked Jim and Dennis if we could drive by the dining hall where I had worked as a young girl. We did. It looked much the same. As we entered Boston proper, I realized this was likely my farewell tour, so I asked if we might also go down Joy Street. Along the sidewalks were all my old friends, still young, still bustling along. They were in new bodies, of course, but I recognized them and waved to some, and they smiled back, though they didn't know me now, so old. Good-bye to all of it. So lovely.

■ ■ ■

Well, I have given you eleven decent chapters, and that may well be enough for you. If you dare venture beyond, be advised that the rest is something of a road book of my travels during the final few years before my hundredth birthday. This section may be of more interest to political organizers than to general readers. So if I leave you here, I would like to thank you very much for letting me share my story. I truly hope it was of some value to you.

Book 2

ON THE ROAD AGAIN

*A*fter Boston we were truly on the road. It was quixotic, but it was the best thing we could think of doing to help, and we were optimistic, as always. We stopped at Yale and camped overnight in a student apartment.

The Yalies were all registered to vote. We were just there for the free room and spaghetti, and to visit Dennis's daughter, Lauren, a junior there. She had just returned from a summer in Guatemala where right-wing gunmen, trying to discourage poor farmers from opposing the disastrous "free trade" agreements, had broken in, put her on the floor with another girl, and threatened them with guns. More recently, some of her friends were just back from being brutalized by the police in Miami over the same issue. Dennis's son, Austin, had recently graduated and was now up in Burlington, working on Howard Dean's campaign. So everyone was doing everything they could. The air was politically charged everywhere, and the conversation around the spaghetti bowl in Lauren's apartment felt like old times on Joy Street.

The next morning, the vehicle was smoking from under the hood as we crossed the Hudson on the Tappan Zee Bridge. From the bridge, you used to be able to look south and see the distant twin towers in Manhattan, but they were two years gone.

Our first working stop was in Easton, Pennsylvania, for the hundredth anniversary of Crayola crayons. We were looking for crowds, and Easton was jumping. Miss Lavender, a hoop-skirted southern belle representing a lovely bipartisan color, helped us at our voter registration table. People of other colors, historical characters, barbershop quartets, and brass bands circled through the town square. It was a very charming beginning for us, and newly signed voter registration forms began to pile up. Miss Lavender told us how her family had long enjoyed good jobs at the Crayola factory and bragged that those jobs had not been exported.

In Bethlehem, an ex-steelworker, now minding a coffee counter because her job had been sent away, told me she didn't need to register to vote because she was through with politics and "sick of the special interests." I asked her which special interests bothered her the most. "Republicans and Democrats," she replied. "Clinton sold our jobs down the river same as the Republicans," she said. "So what's the use?"

After a few days in Philadelphia, walking the downtown streets with volunteers and reporters, including a crew from the BBC, we headed to Gettysburg for some voter registration on campus, a speech, and an overnight stay with Professor Lou and Patricia Hammond. They were at the time rearranging their lives to create an intentional community, an eco-village, really, with their extended family on a tree farm.

Lou and Patricia had both walked with me when I arrived in Washington, and were arrested and jailed with me when we tried to read the Declaration of Independence at the Capitol. We were also in the pokey with John Moyers, who is Bill's son and a progressive publisher, and John Passacantando, later the head of Greenpeace. Lou cut his lip badly in the arrest and languished in a cell for many hours without medical attention. He joked about it as we reminisced. Their warm kitchen, on a hill above the frosty battlefields of Gettysburg, was a good place to talk about the coming election. We left the next morning with a supply of apples and cashews.

Jim had already headed home, so Dennis and I drove across Pennsylvania, making college stops along the length of that huge state. We caught up with the fall colors and counted the horse carts of the Amish. Dennis, driving, called to me as I was organizing Pennsylvania voting forms in the back. I heard him say he thought he would like a tattoo. I perched on the passenger seat and told him that he might think so now, but he might regret it someday. "And your Maureen might not like it," I added.

"Really, Doris? A cashew?" I had misheard him. My hearing was becoming a growing difficulty. I went back to replace the tiny batteries — and to find the cashews from Gettysburg.

And so it went. It seemed that every town was filled with students and activists eager to make a difference in the coming election. As we moved between meetings and events, I took names and email addresses and got a sense of the local groups. We found many organizations already active. It was our job to add energy, recruit new volunteers for them, inspire good news coverage, and move on.

After Pittsburgh we traveled to West Virginia, Virginia, and the length of North Carolina, working with activists at each stop, each city hall, each radio, television, and newspaper office, each university where we could find an opening.

In late November we rolled into Asheville, engine still smoking of course—we had already lost one volunteer driver who was sure the whole vehicle would become a fireball any moment. We put him on a plane home and bought a few fire extinguishers.

In Asheville, we hoped to find some artists to help put some color and graphics on our vehicle.

Blue, a twenty-three-year-old tattoo artist in Asheville, volunteered to organize the effort. She was over six feet in her blue fedora, slim, with vivid blue-green eyes, a little sterling nose ring, small silver rings in the sides of her ears, short, dark hair that she styled herself— featuring a long, narrow strand curling down from each temple. Just below her collarbone, where a Hindu pendant of the elephant god Ganesha would sometimes hang, was a nickel-size blue tattoo: the androgynous symbol of the planet Mercury—the standard female symbol plus two horns atop. Her smile struck me as unusually confident and serene for her age. Tattoos were her living, but she was also a fine painter. Her other interest was energy healing, for which she carried a kit of herbs, oils, and scents.

A few days later, a painting of Rosie the Riveter was perfectly executed across the port side of our vehicle. The starboard side featured the historic march of women for the vote—with straw-hatted me in the parade. "Working Women Vote!" was bannered above the paintings. On the rear was the beginning of what would become two bluebirds holding up a New Hampshire "Live Free or Die" banner. "Vote, Dammit!" was emblazoned across the high front window. The cab was now bright blue; the big side mirror struts were bright yellow. The colors were as stunning as the designs. I was sure the old engine would run fine now: I knew that my old body felt much better with a fresh coat of paint, so why not Rocinante?

The artists were not quite finished when the time came for us to go. Blue was painting in the icy rain, drying a spot before each brushstroke.

Don't worry, I told her, artists in Florida, our next big destination, could finish up. She didn't like that idea at all.

"Maybe I could travel with you for a few days," she said. "I could finish the painting and see a little of Florida." We agreed.

In our multicolor dream van — now more Rosie than Rocinante — we headed south: a gay tattoo artist from the South, a middle-aged organizer from Arizona, and ninety-three-year-old New England me.

ALLIGATORS, MERMAIDS, ETCETERA

13

*W*e drove that night through the rest of North and all of South Carolina, through Georgia, through the coming and going of military towns and their radio stations with callers getting ready to go to Iraq or just coming back from Iraq, or having family in Iraq, and everybody full of pride and patriotism. No one seemed concerned that it was the wrong country to attack, as most countries are.

The engine's overheating and stalling was always curable with a stop for coffee or a few slower miles on side roads under trees decorated with the stars of the Milky Way. The farther we traveled, the more the trees were draped in Spanish moss.

In Gainesville, as Dennis and I worked college events, Blue painted the vehicle. Watching, she became interested in our work. When the crowds were sometimes too big for Dennis and me, she pitched in. She proved to be a natural with a clipboard. We were now finally hitting across the spectrum of generations. In young crowds, she could get the most new voters. In the evenings, she was pumping me for information about politics. She wanted to know everything, and she asked smart questions. And she massaged my old legs.

After a few days it was clear she was reluctant to go home—we offered to fly her, of course. She wanted to stay a few more days and learn more, "If y'all don't mind."

When we were far from volunteers, we had to spring for motel rooms. Blue and I would share the room, and Dennis would sleep in the vehicle. We were happy Gypsies.

It was suddenly Christmas. My friend Nancy Brown, a Portsmouth teacher, came to spend Christmas with Blue and me while Dennis flew home to Arizona.

When he returned, we went right back to work. We met up with local voting groups at a big mall and combed the stores for new voters.

Young clerks were particularly ready to sign up. We tested language: "We're bringing voter forms through the stores as a convenience to employees" got better acceptance than "Would you like to register to vote?" which was like a solicitation instead of a convenience. Blue suggested we take the forms in shopping totes, not on clipboards, to avoid conflict with mall security. We put our lessons on the website and sent an email report to several thousand volunteers, asking them to start cruising the malls, and here's how to do it. Many started sending us reports of their successes.

At an Orlando alligator park, I was to take over the job of an eighteen-year-old, khaki-shorted, ponytailed girl named Jamie. Her job was alligator feeder. To do that, one stands in the mud and throws huge hunks of raw meat to swarms of giant alligators, sometimes inches away, all around you.

Dennis assured me that it was reasonably safe, or at least that I would die a hero. We walked across the alligator lagoons on wooden walkways.

"Do you see the size of them?" I whispered out loud.

"They are gorgeous," Blue said. Nancy Brown was wide-eyed.

Dennis attempted to calm me by asking our host, Tim, the head ranger, if an alligator had killed anyone recently.

"Recently . . . how recently? Well, not exactly killed," he said. A longtime employee had lost a leg and part of his face recently. But he was not killed. Not entirely.

We came to the end of the walkway, to a mud beach where a golf cart soon arrived with a dozen five-gallon buckets of horse meat, each piece as big as three or four steaks. Then the press arrived: two TV stations and the *Orlando Sentinel*.

Two rangers held long sticks to protect me from any gator that might charge, though I didn't imagine a stick would stop a hungry, thousand-pound alligator. The men slapped the water with the sticks, which then started to boil with alligators—more than I could count. They began to crawl up the mud bank rapidly toward me with their big jaws snapping.

So I began tossing hunks of meat, and hoped I could do so fast enough to stop their advances. Tim shouted that I might do it a little faster, please. The meat was heavy and got heavier.

Blue registered Jamie to vote while I flung the meat and while television cameras rolled and while a pretty young reporter for the *Sentinel* tried to interview me. My answers may have been a little short.

The water still boiled as the monsters, tails flipping, water spraying, giant jaws snapping sharp teeth, swarmed ever closer around me. The scene could only have been improved with Chinese gongs and Irish fiddles. Tim, whose white mustache and khaki safari suit made him look positively British, presided calmly over the bloody battle, unfazed by the fact that we were surrounded and outnumbered. He knew we would win if our ammunition held.

Later over lunch with Tim and newly registered Jamie, we learned about alligator wrestling, which Jamie was just learning.

"Do they have you practice with little ones or giant beanbags or what?" I asked her.

"No, you just get in and do it, but you have to be real careful," she said. Tim nodded as he ate.

Well, I suppose so. Later, we dropped her and big Tim off at the park, took farewell pictures, and went into the souvenir shop to purchase a two-foot rubber alligator, which we wired onto Rosie as a hood ornament. Blue named him Tim. The radiator gator would prove a good people magnet in the housing projects and slums ahead. It also gave passing motorists something to look at besides the smoke coming from the hood and, well, everything else.

We drove west out of Orlando, leaving behind wonderful newspaper and television stories about how young people and working women needed to register to vote and where they could do it, and that if this old woman, who was born ten years before women could vote, cared that much, then they should care, too. They should do it to value the sacrifices made.

Well, "sacrifice" is the undervalued word in our politics today. It's why my walk worked, why risking it with alligators works, and why the bigger and more serious campaigns of history, such as those of Gandhi and Martin Luther King Jr., were so successful. And it is the main reason unsuccessful campaigns fail. You certainly don't have to, and shouldn't, set yourself afire, but you should demonstrate that the issue is worth your own respectable pain and suffering. Otherwise, why should anyone bother rearranging the status quo? And I'm not sure that marching around Washington on weekends, when everyone has gone anyway, or going to jail en masse really does the trick anymore. As King did, you really have to stand in the way of evil and take your licks, showing the world the moral bankruptcy of the corruption you would end.

Well, we were far from all that, but it had been a fine day, starting at a Waffle House where I was "hon," and where the waitresses and the manager, when they asked about our vehicle and learned about our mission, insisted that voting was a waste of time. One waitress followed us out to the parking lot to register. "Don't mind them, they're registered all right, but sometimes I wish they wasn't," she said. "Sign here, hon," I replied.

Motel maids had earlier signed the small stack of forms accumulating on the morning's clipboard. Now we had Jamie, who had registered as a Republican. Well, that was fine.

It was January 5, 2004. Attorney General Ashcroft had recently recused himself from the investigation into the outing of CIA agent Valerie Plame. Kerry's campaign was doing well. Bush was all over the newspapers, pushing his No Child Left Behind program. I read newspapers as we drove, bringing articles up to Dennis from time to time to read aloud.

My emphysema was kicking up, especially after the heavy lifting of horse parts. Sometimes my coughing coincided with Rosie's. Sometimes we both needed a nap under roadside trees.

Mermaids were next. I would be a mermaid, so that all mermaids might someday vote.

As late as the 1970s, Florida was the land of family auto vacations. Millions of families in station wagons buzzed like honeybees from roadside attraction to attraction: Marineland, Gatorworld, other marine, jungle, and alligator parks, rollercoaster piers, beaches, and a circus town. There were over two hundred major roadside attractions.

Walt Disney World and Epcot changed all that by making a complex of parks in a single, fly-in, fly-out destination. The older roadside attractions and the communities they supported have ever since been sadly fading. In retailing terms, Disney built a Wal-Mart.

Gatorworld—Jamie and Tim's park—seemed to be surviving. It was more fun than Walt Disney World—which I had visited over

Christmas—because everything in the little gator park was very real. There was a feeling of love, commitment, and courage there. Jamie's plans were to study animals in college. She particularly loved gators, even after one had eaten her dog.

We were now headed to a mermaid park on the Gulf Coast that, for 1950s quirky charm, had them all beat: Weeki Wachee Springs, the City of Mermaids.

The park had suffered financially until the little town around it purchased the property out of receivership and treated it like a city park with benefits—the benefits being mermaids. The water-park elements—big slides and swimming pools—are available to the kids of the town every summer day. The adjoining City of Mermaids, maintained as a campy tourist attraction, provides youth jobs and tax revenue to the tiny community. The jobs—mermaids and mermen—very literally beat the pants off the McDonald's and Wendy's jobs suffered by other American teens.

The park is built on a natural phenomenon—a spring that delivers up millions of gallons of freshwater each day. It rushes into a huge, glass-walled theater where the mer-people perform classics such as Hans Christian Andersen's "The Little Mermaid." They mime it to an announcer's narration. Because the water is a chilly seventy-two degrees, the performers can't stay long in the water. And as the spring is the headwaters of the Weeki Wachee River, alligators sometimes wiggle upstream and pirouette into the show. The boys and girls take a break.

When the mermaids first appear in the water, the effect on the children in the audience, who watch through a great bank of underwater windows, is electric. "Watch the little girls, especially," Barbara, a long-time mermaid—sans fin—advised me before the show. Yes, their eyes popped wide soon enough.

The spring is real, the gators are real, and how about the mermaids? In a sense, they are. The whole thing has become a lifestyle for many of them. Former mermaids, even into their seventies, come back monthly to swim under the waves with each other and remember who they are. They mentor the young mermaids and mermen and have a true fellowship of the fin. So I say they are real. I asked Barbara if she is a real mermaid: "You know, it kind of is the real me," she explained.

I imagined how wonderful it would be if my old friends from my youth could still come together often like that. How lovely it would be to see them. We would keep each other going, wouldn't we?

It was no small thing for the mermaids to take me into their inner sanctum and fit me with a beautiful, shimmering blue-green mermaid skin. I came out in the arms of a handsome fellow who set me down in a chair in front of the great performance windows. An unregistered mermaid with a pink fin and a fine front was set beside me. Gorgeous mermaids suddenly filled the window behind us, stretching out an American flag in the deep water as patriotic music played to the auditorium full of confused tourists. A clipboard appeared, and I registered the mermaid beside me. Behind us in the water, the submerged mermaids began registering each other using grease pencils on laminated registration forms clipped to neon-colored plastic clipboards, all prepared by Blue. It was the world's first underwater voter registration event. Two television stations and one major daily newspaper from Tampa and St. Pete caught it all.

The sheriff, the mayor, all the local and county dignitaries were on hand. The county registrar of voters was all over the reporters with information on registration locations. She said they were going to put together some workplace voter registration events, thanks to this encouragement.

I took one more look at the great window and waved good-bye to the mermaids, who waved back, their long hair flowing so beautifully around their smiles. We bought a little mermaid statuette for the dashboard and headed south, where activist volunteers in St. Petersburg had plans for us.

In St. Pete, we bought a little red wagon for me to pull down the city streets with voter forms. It had a voter registration sign popping up from it, and clipboards and water bottles, sunscreen and a map. I went up and down streets, flanked by young volunteers, traversing the city. Television and newspaper reporters followed along. We ended the walk at the University of South Florida with a voter registration rally.

Here is a piece of the speech, so you can see what that sort of thing was like:

I hope you are not taking your studies here just so that you can be someday comfortably secure as somebody's wife, somebody's husband, somebody's employee, somebody's taxpayer. I hope you feel within your heart a spark of life that is far greater than any of that. For here you are in a world, and at a time, where heroes are required. You may not quite see that. It may not impress you that the polar ice lost 44 percent of its thickness in the last forty years . . . that there may be great dislocations of people, great famines, great epidemics.

You may not see exactly what I see when I say our democracy, our freedoms, are melting away, too, and that even a few years ago when you were born, an American citizen had the right to a lawyer and an appearance before a judge, and all that is melting away. You may think that the inconveniences at the airport are unavoidable, when they are the direct result of a foreign policy that has favored our corporations at the expense of the American people's values of peace, world democracy, and economic fairness. You pay billions now to subsidize the primary and secondary effects of the unbridled greed of a new class of globalized robber barons, and heroes are required if we are to have the resources to care for each other, to educate our children, to provide for our health, to secure our free and happy lives under our own healthy trees and under our own free and safe skies.

I am not exaggerating when I say that a heroic life is called for, and that you must rise to that call if you are to live in a good world. And this heroism begins with simple acts of faith such as voting.

Well, that was quite negative, looking back. It's better to motivate with positive thoughts when you can. I can see some of my own lessons learned coming through that speech: don't waste your creative life to become some domestic servant or corporate cog.

We camped at the home of Winnie and Al Foster in St. Pete. It was during this time that Blue seemed to open up to me. I learned a great deal about her youth, and about the difficulties she struggled to overcome. I watched her grow more responsible every day, helping us to organize and think ahead. We had been planning a few days or a week in advance; she now calendared the month ahead, which helped immensely. Each evening she walked down to the bay to watch for the great manatees in the water there. She stared at the star-sprinkled black water for hours and was clearly moving through something important. People have to feel emotionally safe before they start asking themselves who they really are and what they are going to do with their lives. Only when they are safe are they free of the defensiveness that prevents them from moving to higher levels of maturity.

We argued now like family. Blue always cut her own hair, sometimes leaving a bathroom looking as if black poodles had exploded. I was hesitant to criticize her in the first weeks and months, but now she was like a grandchild, or, actually, like one of my old Boston pals. Anything could be said. Blue would criticize in return, but with great southern diplomacy.

At the Florida Citrus Festival, midstate, Blue perfected what she called her "apathy-matching" voter registration technique. She signed up all the carnies—they would have jumped off the top of the Ferris wheel for her. Apathy matching has to do with assessing the attitude of the person you are approaching. For registering carnies, it was "Hey, want to help me out by doing something useless?" That would get her a conversation, a signature, and a promise to vote. "You know, as Americans, it's important that we waste our time this way, don't you agree?" She would look at them very seriously, and they would laugh and agree. She would brilliantly cut through their cynicism to find their little stash of patriotism.

I couldn't help but feel that we were something of a sideshow ourselves. We weren't really registering that many people. I hoped we were making a difference, and we were getting good reports from people on our lists, but progress was hard to see. We were certainly a very marginal operation, and it was expensive to be on the road and running a mobile communications and public relations operation—much more so than just walking across the country. Maybe we should go home. Dennis suggested we go for a Saturday drive to think it through.

We stopped on a red dirt road in an endless orange grove—so big that it seemed like you could see the curvature of the earth down the rows. There wasn't another soul anywhere. I picked an orange and ate it. Others present may have done the same, but I am no snitch.

If we owe something to the Florida Orange Growers Association, however, let me say by way of testimonial that Florida oranges are quite delicious, and they did perk up our spirits and change our luck.

In fact, less than a mile down that same road, we came across an African American man, retirement age, under a big straw hat at a junction. He was selling something out of a steaming, charcoal-fired vat. We were the only possible customers as far as we could see. God had put him there just for us.

"Ain't you ever et a boiled peanut?" he asked.

You might think this was a poor old fellow who lives in a shack somewhere and scratches out a living selling some little soulful treat. That would be the old South; this was the new. Mr. Roberts was a retired engineer, selling boiled peanuts in a little partnership with his brother. We had just beat the crowd.

The peanuts are boiled in the shell, swelling to twice their size like a little body too long in a swamp. Fresh from the cauldron, they are coated in a thick broth of meaty, Cajun flavors. You pop them out of their dripping shells into your mouth. They are wonderful, like big, beefy, Boston baked beans.

"I'm in Boston!" I said. "It's wonderful!"

"Lady, you a long way from that place."

Mr. Roberts was an angel beside the road.

"Well, look, you need to be working with the churches down here. That's what you got to do," he said, after we talked for a while and he let me share my worries.

"That way, they have the church committees to keep the registration going after you and your friends are on your way."

He rattled off the names of several pastors who weren't afraid to get political. Dennis took notes and asked Mr. Roberts if he might call ahead for us. He said he would do it right then. He found his cell phone in a deep pocket of his overalls and called the first church, his own.

The next morning, a rainy Sunday, we were the honored guests at the Faith Pentecostal Church in Avon Park. The music and energy as we walked in were inspirational beyond my ability to fully describe. I was honored for my age alone. They already had been told what I had done in my past. I don't know how they knew, as they were all just arriving as we were, but they did.

Blue and I looked like a million dollars. Tall in her Sunday best, her temple twirls coming down from her blue fedora, her little chest tattoo showing between her lapels, our Blue was suddenly a supermodel. We were escorted to the front row. Dennis was also in his Sunday best.

The Pentecostals, once called the Holy Rollers, know how to find divinity and joy in the present moment—with every clap of the hand, with spontaneous dancing and uninhibited expressions of joy. Though we were of a different race and belief, several ministers welcomed us from the pulpit and, with voices of awesome authority, blessed our mission.

We were asked to come up front and be blessed, which we did. Pastor Brown and his wife, both among the best speakers I have ever heard, weaved the Gospel into politics, while the choir and the band found the right places to come in and make it all rise up to the roof every few minutes.

"Granny D, you come up and speak to us right now," the reverend's wife called. Like all the women in the big church, she wore a fancy, big hat and a flowing, bright dress.

I was ecstatic and too moved to speak; I pushed Dennis forward. He talked for a minute about my long walk, my going to jail, my use of Dr. King's and Mohandas Gandhi's five principles of nonviolent change—that we must bring change to the world not by making others suffer, but by suffering ourselves. I nodded sagely.

"That's right!" the people said, led by Pastor Brown. The choir was building a holy background hum.

"As our Lord suffered!" Mrs. Brown added. "Hallelujah! Glory, glory!" people shouted.

Then I stepped forward. I told them we had met so many people who had given up on voting because they believed politicians don't care about the people anymore—and there is so much despair.

"That's right!" several called out. "Amen, sister!" And the choir did something big to go along with it.

I said things would never change until all the people used the power of the vote—used it to reward and used it to punish—used the main power of free people, a power that so many had sacrificed so much to get.

"That's right! That's right!" Pastor Brown moved in and took it from there, as the choir swelled. They all got to singing and dancing—it was something. Pastor Brown said that the people stopped voting when the politicians stopped caring about regular people, but "everybody got to vote" as an act of faith in the future.

"Everybody got to vote" he commanded on behalf of the Lord. "Everybody got to vote!" he danced.

People were dancing to the idea, and the choir took it up to the rafters a couple times more. Before he was done, Pastor Brown had pointed to a young lady who was going to set up the tables for registration, and she would be in charge of all that until the election.

In the back of the church after the service, it was all cookies and hugs and introductions to children and grandmothers.

The peanut man had set us right. Down the rest of the road we would check in with the Gospel churches, and sometimes, like that morning, it was something.

I think it took us a whole week to come down from that morning. We had the spirit. We drove back to St. Pete by way of Peace River and a calm lake where we three paused to let things sink in before we went back to work.

We stopped later that evening in a diner that was once the favorite gathering place and sort-of town hall for Gibsonton, a community made prosperous by men and women of unusual countenance—they had been circus sideshow attractions. Al the Giant (eight-foot-four) and his wife, Jeanie the Half-Girl (two-foot-six) settled there in the early 1940s, and other professional peers came to live there over the years, including Lobster Boy and Percila the Monkey Girl. The post office has a counter for midgets. We were in heaven: great food and the most interesting clippings all over the menus and walls. Blue was ready to move there, and what she was feeling was tremendous warmth for all things human—the place glowed with love.

If the Florida Democratic Party would make its headquarters there, they would begin to understand politics, and the world would surely be on the mend. The people of this sorry world need respect, love, and community. The hungrier they are for it, the more beautiful it is when they finally find it. We are all deformed and beautiful, all backward in some things and geniuses in others, and only the roundness of community can bring it all together.

Then it was back across the bay to Winnie and Al's embrace in St. Pete. Winnie maneuvered us into the Martin Luther King Day Parade.

With Rosie as a moving supply depot, Blue at the wheel, Dennis and I worked the crowds on both sides of the parade street, three and four people deep, all reaching out for registration forms as if they were hundred-dollar bills. Some asked for stacks for their churches.

I had been hurting. I had morning pains in my back, and my breathing had become difficult. Blue gave me a massage that morning to get me ready for the long parade, which I literally ran—zipping back and forth from the crowds to the vehicle for more forms. I was as fit as a teen that day.

Before we left the Tampa–St. Pete area, a new idea was for us to hit fast-food joints after the busy dinner hours, and, sure enough, we found eighteen- and nineteen-year-olds behind the counters who were ready and eager to register. We got the word out to our national volunteers: hit the burger joints between rush hours.

One evening, making our way down a Tampa sidewalk, we passed in front of a big place that looked like a restaurant of some kind. "What about this place?" I asked Dennis.

"If I go in there, Doris. I'll never hear the end of it. It's a strip joint."

"They're working women, aren't they?" I replied.

"You're on your own," he said, and parked himself on a low wall—Blue was elsewhere on a mission. So I went in.

I walked right in, past the disoriented bouncer and cashier.

Well, it was quite a show. I came out about an hour later, flanked by a small crew of fully dressed but obviously well-cast ladies. They thanked me for coming. I had voter signatures from the women inside and some of the customers. They asked how else they could help. I suggested they keep voter forms in the dressing room and send some to the other clubs, which they agreed to do. They said they were going to set up a website, "Exotic Women Vote," which they actually later did. They gave me a shirt with the name of the club embroidered discreetly.

"I know you'll never wear it," one of them said.

I wore it the next morning for a live television interview, just to send them some respect.

■ ■ ■

Blue left us. She said she had an opportunity to catch a ride to Asheville and needed to go back for a while. I understood completely, or thought I did. She said she would return, but I seriously doubted that.

That evening it was sad with her gone. Dennis and I had dinner quietly in the vehicle. She had talked a lot to him lately, and sometimes my hearing wasn't good enough to catch it. I asked him what she had said about going back, and if she would be all right.

"She doesn't have an ounce of BS in her," Dennis said. "If she says she's coming back, she will. But she doesn't want to be like the little kid on this trip, with us buying her meals and everything. She has an opportunity in Asheville to paint a mural for some pretty good money. She is going to do that so she can come back and pay her own way, and we can travel as equals. That's what she told me, and I believe her."

■ ■ ■

In Fort Myers, we went straight to a neighborhood we were warned not to go to. We parked steaming Rosie in the middle of a rough housing project and started visiting with the people who were hanging out on patios, talking on cell phones, making plans for the evening, and doing little drug deals. Veronica Shoemaker, an elderly African American florist, whose shop is located at the edge of the district, had given us the lay of the land as she arranged flowers — she was busy, as it was almost Valentine's Day. Her shop is on Veronica Shoemaker Boulevard, named in honor of her long activism. We were there to get her advice and so that Dennis could send valentine flowers home.

"Just go do it. I can't tell you more than that. Nobody is going to eat you up," she said.

We went in. We talked to mothers about their sons who were in prison or who were out, but had records hanging over them. They couldn't get decent jobs and couldn't vote. Some of the women had seen me on the TV news that morning, as we had done an interview on the way into town. The telephone grapevine quickly spread through the projects. One after another, young men came by for instructions on how to get their voting rights restored. Dennis had put together stapled kits of the right forms.

We let the little kids pet Tim the Alligator on the hood and have a peek inside the vehicle, which might as well have been the starship *Enterprise*.

"You got a refrigerator! What you got in there? You got any pop?" A hundred times.

Several mothers appointed themselves to get more forms and make sure they were filled out and mailed properly. They started brainstorming about who had recently turned eighteen, and who would do so before the election. I wished dearly that we had found someone locally to keep up the energy and attention. Again we wondered where on earth the Democratic Party was. They would be smart to close up their office downtown and put it right here.

Jim showed up in Fort Myers to see how I was doing. He took us out to Sanibel Island, were I saw the most stunning sunset ever in my life. It was good to stand in the sand with him and look at all that beauty together. Here he was a retired man. I had been given the blessing of watching him through nearly his whole life now, as I had seen all of my beautiful daughter's life. It hurts, of course, to see it all, and know that it ends, but the beauty of seeing it is a blessing.

He drove ahead of us as we traveled Alligator Alley toward the biggest target of our Florida project: Miami.

14

WAKE UP AND LIVE

*F*rom Miami, Jim, who knows Florida very well and goes there alone each year to recharge his batteries and give his New England skin a needed sunlight therapy, headed south into the Keys, and we went into Little Haiti after saying good-bye in Miami.

In the nearly two weeks it took us to organize south of Tampa, through Fort Myers, across Alligator Alley, and around to Miami, Blue had been doing what she said she would do. In Miami, following our Internet postings, she found us. She had completed the mural and now had the money to feel like the adult she had lately become. Jim got to meet her before he left. He had distrusted her until he finally met her and hugged her.

"Ah, darlin'," he said, "you stink!" She had driven the eight hundred miles from Asheville straight through in an old car that would be useful for volunteers to use ahead of us. She laughed, and they were now instant friends. "Wonderful!" he whispered to me. It never takes him long to size someone up, and he always gets it right.

After Jim left, Dennis thought we should have a cocktail in South Beach to celebrate Blue's return and to stiffen ourselves for Little Haiti. We certainly did.

Little Haiti is not a slum, but is a hard place compared with South Beach — though more joyful. We could smell its Caribbean restaurants and hear its music as we drove in, the rich white sand of South Beach still sparkling on our tires.

Brightly painted buildings, Creole kitchens, beauty salons, music stores, and car repair shops are strung along the main streets of Little Haiti. Behind the commercial streets are little homes and two-story housing projects. The broadcast from the Creole-language radio station blares from screened doorways and from passing cars. The office of the Haitian American Society stands at the heart of the community.

We cruised, attracting suspicious glances from the hundreds of people walking along the streets and hanging out on corners. It is odd to come into a new community without much of a plan, knowing we will get many of these people to vote, knowing we will leave with many new friends, but not yet imagining how we will do it. "We are samurai" and "trust the force" were Dennis's only explanations for it. Blue would correct him: "Ninjas."

We found a cheap motel and settled in for the night. Before I turned in, I looked out the window and saw Dennis reading in the vehicle. There were still people walking on the sidewalks, some obviously plying their trades. We were a long way from home, and it was one of those moments when you wonder what you are doing there. It just seems silly and a little pathetic sometimes.

The usual morning would see Dennis knocking at the motel room door with coffee and muffins. Blue would still be asleep, cuddled like a cat in her bed and unready for light or humans; I would be bent over a book, or a sheaf of news articles that had come off the printer in the vehicle, or a speech draft for down the road. I would have my hearing aids still on the night table. As I always seemed to have my back to the door for better reading light from the window, there was nothing I could do to avoid being completely startled by Dennis. After that big morning jump, we would laugh, and I would go scurry for my hearing aids so we could talk about the plan for the day. Getting Blue up would be the first big project, especially that first morning after she had driven so far to come back to us.

We found the big Catholic church and introduced ourselves to the pastor, a Father Dabus, pronounced "Daboo," who was a quiet Haitian man of great dignity. Our inquiries to patrons at a coffee shop had identified him as the man to meet. He listened with suspicion and eventually warmed to us, but he voiced his concern:

"People had a bad time voting here last time," he told us. Indeed, stories of voter intimidation had been following us all over Florida. He told of police arrests in polling places and soldiers posted to keep people in the housing projects.

"I will call Jimmy Carter and ask him to send poll watchers here for the next election," I offered.

"You know Carter?" Father Dabus leaned forward on his desk.

"I do." It wasn't much of a stretcher, as Carter had reviewed my first book in glowing terms. I had run into him in Seattle recently, and he was so warm that, under these circumstances, I felt he might actually help if I sent up a flare.

Beyond our view, other, much larger efforts were under way to do the same thing; an army of poll watchers was in the making.

Father Dabus looked at the draft of the flyer we intended to distribute around Little Haiti. It said that if the Haitians in Miami were ever to be as powerful as the Cubans, they must all become voters, plus it had some nice words about democracy and civic responsibility. Father Dabus liked the Cuban part. "But this should all be in Creole," he suggested, sliding it back to me. Did I think I could find a good translator? I assured him we could. I didn't want to ask him for little things when we wanted to ask him yet for a big thing.

The big thing: yes, he agreed to promote voter registration from the pulpit and have a committee set up to register parishioners, which was another way of saying almost everybody in Little Haiti would soon be registered. We then met with the Catholic Social Charities people, in whose offices some five hundred people are served every day. They agreed to stack up the forms and our new flyers, once we had them translated and printed. They were agreeable mostly because Father Dabus had called ahead. It was like that all day. We took some afternoon time to park under a tree so I could start the call to Jimmy Carter and also get my nap.

When I emerged from the vehicle after a little rest, a Haitian woman in a bright, flowing dress approached me and said she had heard about this Granny D and would like to help us. I asked if she knew anyone who could translate our flyer into Creole. Yes, she could do it herself, as she taught both languages. "Father Dabus sent you?" I asked.

"Yes, yes! Father Daboo!" she laughed and gave me a little hug.

Later that night we had our flyer, but only after a lecture from her in a coffee place near her house.

"The more I tried to do this," she said, "the more wrong I knew it was. You need to talk more about the issues of this place," she advised. She gave us a quick lesson in the hot issues of Little Haiti that could be improved with a bit more democracy. More about schools. More about the dread condition of the housing projects where many Little Haiti residents live—then, after that, we could ice the cake with the Cuban argument about political power.

As she talked I remembered how, when walking into Memphis on my long walk, I had asked Dick Gregory, who was holding my hand as we crossed the bridge, how I might get poor African Americans behind campaign finance reform. He squeezed my hand and said, "Granny D, if your children have rats in their bedroom, or not enough to eat, or bad schools or crime outside, that's all you think about. Don't ask poor people to think too far past the problems right in front of them." I was now feeling like we were slow learners. We should have had a better flyer to start with in Little Haiti. But she fixed it up for us.

Now we had a flyer to help us work the neighborhoods, housing projects, beauty salons, barber shops, laundries, and little markets— nearly all of which were dilapidated but brightly painted in pure colors. One side of the flyer had our main message; the other side promoted a citizenship and voting registration event that coming Saturday, where people could practice using the voting machines and get signed up. The event had already been organized, but we could help provide the crowd. In arriving just before that event, our timing, as usual, was spookily perfect.

"It's called synchronicity," Blue explained over a spaghetti dinner in the vehicle, then going on about the teachings of Carl Gustav Jung, from a book she had borrowed from Dennis.

By day, people led us to apartments where someone had just turned eighteen, or where someone had just become a citizen, and they often served as translators for us. The mothers always got it, and became our agents throughout the projects.

In the evenings we cruised the main streets in the vehicle, trying to hand out the flyers to people on street corners. Often they were suspicious and shied away, even after we had the Creole radio stations talking about us. Our big stacks of flyers were not thinning fast enough.

After a particularly discouraging evening of that, we stopped and I cooked a wonderful soup for dinner. Dennis looked out and saw a couple of shops he thought might help us.

After dinner, we ducked first into a used record store right in front of where we were parked. We explained our mission and our problem to the young clerk. What is the best music that says liberation, political freedom? He didn't have to think. "You mean Bob Marley?" I thought he would say Bob Marley, but I was afraid to suggest him, as it might just be a stereotype. You should always ask anyway.

"Marley. Yes, Marley is the one people listen to and believe, because he speaks for people, you know? He is the man, you know? Always Marley, you know?"

Dennis got out his wallet. "Keep your money!" the young clerk said, smiling.

We rigged our public address system, used normally for speeches at rallies, to blare Marley from the high windows of Rosie's sleeping loft. While Blue finished the rewiring, Dennis and I went into a little souvenir shop in the same strip. Its window displayed a Republic of Haiti flag and a pile of old toys and trinkets for sale. It was dark but the door was half open. Inside, candles were burning in a circle on the floor, and an old woman, in the center of them, was clearly in the middle of a Voodoo ritual. We apologized. She said it was not a problem and, standing, said that she would help us. She went immediately into the back of the store and came out with a folded Haitian flag—a very big and beautiful new one.

"Here it is. Why do you need this flag?" she asked.

We had not mentioned a flag, but it is indeed what we had gone there to buy. I told her why we were in town.

"Take it, then. I give it to you because you are trying to do a good thing."

Dennis tied it so it would flow from the rear of the vehicle—and nearly as big as the vehicle. Then we rolled out again.

Blue hung out the passenger window, and I occupied the open dinette window with handfuls of flyers. We cruised slowly with Bob Marley blaring.

The same people who had viewed us with suspicion an hour earlier now began to move, to dance and smile, rocking up to the vehicle to get their flyers.

"Creole!" they noticed instantly on the flyer: "Very nice, very nice!" The headline was "Poukisa Ayisyen dwe Vote?"—Why should Haitians vote? Its tone was influenced by Blue's technique of apathy matching, perfected a long way back on the road.

"Mama be jammin' tonight!" a man sang as he danced up to take some flyers from my hand. Blue recruited the young men at her window to take stacks to the beauty parlors and little stores she pointed out to them. Like her bees, they came back for more, always dancing to the music with great smiles and shaking her little white hand. Many didn't know much English, but they had known the English lyrics of Marley all their lives.

The bright yellow buildings had turned neon green under the street-lights. The air was cool and scented with pungent spice. Smiling faces kept coming out of the dark for flyers. The bigger-than-life faces of Martin Luther King Jr. and Haitian president Jean-Bertrand Aristide loomed large on murals painted in unexpected places. Blue would run a stack of flyers into a market or a beauty salon, whose customers and owners stared from windows. Three young men walking under a free-way bridge changed their walking to dancing as we approached and as the music filled the concrete space. Fists flew up as they turned and smiled: "We gonna register, Mama!" one shouted to us as we passed.

By the end of the evening, Little Haiti was primed for the Saturday voter registration event, which was a great day, with overflowing crowds attending. And the church and social agency were stocked with voting forms and helpful attitudes.

From that night onward, we could not cruise those streets without some people waving fists in the air and shouting "Mama!" to me.

If the Democratic Party had a storefront in such places, and if it advocated for such communities by being inside them, it would be a different world. We couldn't find the party anywhere, except in the person of Jacques Despinosse, vice mayor of North Miami, who let us set up in his business office there in Little Haiti. We wanted to con-nect with as many community groups as possible, to see that there would be a continuing registration effort after we left. He was the political man of Little Haiti—well dressed, highly educated, with a front office filled with plaques and photos of his Democratic Party connections. All day, people came in to talk to this godfather of the district. He gave us the names of all the people we must talk to, and lent us vacant desks and phones to do so. For a few days at least, we were the Democratic Party.

Toward the end of the afternoon—it was Wednesday, February 25, 2004—there was a strange mood in the office. People were talking excitedly in Creole on the phone and leaving early. Looking out the window, I could see little clusters of people gathering on the street. "What is going on?" I asked Jacques's receptionist, who was busy locking her files.

"Aristide!" she said. "Aristide!" And she hurried outside.

We stopped our work and were on the sidewalk when Jacques, terribly excited and serious, came bounding in high steps across the street from somewhere: "Follow me!" he shouted to us, "History, history!"

Directly across were the offices of the Haitian American Society and a street-window meeting room that quickly filled with the respected leaders of Little Haiti. We stayed in an anteroom, watching through glass doors as they entered an aerobic discussion in Creole. Jacques was most animated, his gold-rimmed glasses and big gold watch flashing around, catching the last rays of the day as they cut into the room. He raised his arms and jabbed a little finger down and down to nail point after point.

Between the coming and going of English and Creole, and from the bits of information arriving from the street, we gathered that Aristide, the popularly elected, ex-Catholic priest and president of Haiti, had been overthrown. Little Haiti has strong pro- and anti-Aristide factions, but that was not quite the issue. It was more immediate. The CIA had done this? "Of course—it is always the CIA in such matters," explained a man who was huddled with us in the anteroom.

The meeting was about the Haitian community's need to speak with one voice, not as factions. Yes, peacekeepers should be sent immediately—that should be demanded, but perhaps not American peacekeepers. What is our position? Men and a few women shuttled in and out of the room, making cell calls on the sidewalk and huddling in twos and threes, then returning to the meeting. What are the facts? There seemed to have been a call from the Miami head of the U.S. Coast Guard a few minutes after five—only an hour earlier—something about a ship in Miami Harbor with armed men aboard. The Coast Guard was approaching the ship. Was it Aristide, or a ship of partisans leaving Miami for Haiti? Or all a rumor? What is our position? People who knew people made calls. Is Aristide coming to Miami? How will we care for him? Where? What is our position? Then long, careful arguments and agreements in Creole and the processing of information from all the personal phone calls made to nephews in the Coast

Guard, and friends of friends in high places, and cousins in Haiti who might know what was going on.

Within an hour something had been resolved; information had been received. Jacques finally emerged, quickly telling us that he was late to teach a class and that all had been resolved; there would be a press conference in the morning, and all of Little Haiti would speak with one voice.

Aristide had, in fact, been kidnapped by the CIA and by U.S. troops at gunpoint and was on his way to Africa. He was getting way too democratic in his reforms. When democracy raises its head in the lands south of the United States, the United States responds because such doings are bad for business. The Bush White House called the report of Aristide's CIA kidnapping "utter nonsense," but it was proved true in the weeks following.

In its hour of uncertainty, the Haitian community had done the one thing it could do: it preserved its unity in the face of a potentially divisive challenge. If I had been a Haitian on that emotional evening, I would have borrowed our vehicle and driven around with the big flag flying and Marley blaring. But we were especially outsiders this night, and so we went away to let them be Haitians. We had done our voter registration thing, and it would continue in the church and in the offices. They had other things to think about right now. A good part of politics is knowing when to come and when to go. We left.

Later that evening we cased Overtown, the African American neighborhood closer to downtown Miami. Dennis had a meeting set for the morning.

Our breakfast was with former gang members getting into a new thing: voting. Two members of the Miami Heat basketball team were eating at the next table; bootleg music and movies were on sale at the side of the room. Over greasy eats, Brian Dennis of Brothers of the Same Mind had some interesting things to say about why the Democrats had been losing elections.

"You got the bad voting machines and the purging of the blacks from the voting lists, and you got that b——, what's her name?" he said. "But you also had Clinton in there. He was so busy triangulatin' that he messed up everything. He put a hundred thousand extra cops on the streets, right? That made the cities safer, right? Well, maybe it did.

But it also meant that every brother driving down any street with a cracked taillight or a twisted license plate was pulled over, and anybody with anything in their cars, like a little weed or the wrong size pocket knife, was going to get hauled in with a felony. I don't know how many tens of thousands of young men lost the right to vote right there, but they were sure as hell Democrats. They were enough, just them in this one city, to turn the 2000 election. So that's what you get for trying to be Republicans," he said. "And probably just as bad in other states, too."

The alternative to that heightened police state, of course, would have been more jobs and better schools and easier college loans, which was his next point.

He told us whom to talk to in Overtown. He got us a spot in a street fair, set for the following morning. I spent the rest of the day pulling the little red wagon through the neighborhoods and into the old downtown area, which feels like Havana with its covered sidewalk archways, family stores, and restaurants. For the street fair, Blue bought a stack of poster boards and a big box of colored markers. We set up a table and let kids make "vote for me" posters. That drew in their parents and their older siblings, and we did a good business registering new voters. Blue also bought a big bag of plastic jewels and let kids glue them onto the vehicle, outlining the flames that she had painted some time earlier to ward off real flames. Old Rosie had become a rolling art project.

After Miami we gave ourselves a two-day working vacation in Key West. Mike Eisner, a Baltimore activist, joined us. There wasn't a spare motel room or RV space anywhere in Key West, so we camped on the beach, which was my hope all along. We had a whiskey before lights out, and, with flashlights, tracked the movements of little octopi and other strange creatures in the tide.

"Where are they going to go?" Blue said as she stirred the water around them. She meant global warming and all that.

We laid our bedding out on the sand and called it a day. The breeze was balmy and perfectly subtle. In the morning we tied a big pirate flag to Rosie's stern and started cruising the neighborhoods of Key West. Old mariners with leathered faces came up from boats and signed. One fellow said he had dropped out of voting years ago but knew he needed to get back in it "before they ruin the whole planet," he said.

Mike and Dennis had a beer while Blue and I worked a street of massage parlors.

Later, we found Jim at a beach. We were standing with him in the water, talking about our adventures to date and strategizing the road ahead when I noticed three sharks not far away and circling closer. I mentioned them to Jim, but he waved them off and continued the meeting. They seemed to be getting quite close. Finally, Jim, maybe for me, said, OK, they are getting pretty close, and we took our leave. Jim is that way. You would want him with you if aliens ever invaded Earth, though he would change the oil and stop for peanuts and white cheddar popcorn before making a run for it.

We made our usual stops at communities along the way, leaving Mike in Miami. Now just the three of us again, we camped and made a fine dinner in a swamp near Cape Canaveral.

On Leap Day, 2004, a Sunday, we limped into Daytona Beach after an unusual number of stops to let the engine cool. We arrived at the beginning of the Sixty-fourth Annual Daytona Beach Bike Week. Down every street were literally thousand of Harleys and other bikes. There were, in fact, six hundred thousand bikers in town. The roar covered the city with a constant drone. At every stoplight two dozen or more bikes quickly surrounded us with riders who looked at us as curiously as we looked at them. Should we keep going, or try to do something with this? They looked pretty rough.

Blue laughed. This was more her crowd. "Trust me, Doris, you're tougher than any of these people," she said. Fine. We'll register them.

We found an inexpensive motel right on the beach, thanks to a whole bike club that had canceled on account of a funeral.

We mixed in on the sidewalks for a while, asking people if they wanted to register to vote, but we might as well have asked them if they wanted to buy life insurance or sign a petition to make helmets mandatory. They were in a party mood, and we didn't look like fun.

"Think of something," I told Dennis and Blue, then I went to bed for the night, after some Chinese takeout.

Overnight, Dennis set up a website, "BikersVote.com," with all the state links to online voter registration. Blue designed, with biker art, a little folding palm card we could give out to promote the site and make the point that people who don't vote are not really free, that other people are bossing them around. They found a twenty-four-hour copy shop, printed up thousands, and showed them to me in the morning. They also had a special shirt printed for me, with an American flag–wrapped skull biker and the words "Register to Vote, You Mothers." It actually used the longer-form word.

While we had been lost on the sidewalks that first day, the second day was quite different: the crowd formed circles around me and signed up as fast as we could push the clipboards around. It was the shirt. We became the stars of the street, as we spread our flyers and filled up ever-fatter clipboards. Everybody wanted to have pictures taken with me.

We naturally worried that we were talking to a crowd that would vote against the stream of our own thinking, but we were soon made wise to the fact that bikers like freedom, and while they weren't crazy about Kerry or Dean, many were angrily opposed to Bush. Bikers include about every kind of American, despite what you might think. A group of lesbian bikers—judging by the messages on their bikes and persons—passed our vehicle one evening, shouting, "Anybody but Bush." Was it so obvious that we were Democrats? I suppose it was.

After a long day on sidewalks that were tattoo-to-tattoo, with Blue happily leading the way, we retired to a big event on the edge of town: a wrestling match that took place in a load of coleslaw the size of the La Brea Tar Pits. It was a women's event. Even with that mighty distraction, people were eager to talk to me, have their pictures taken, and agreed to spread around our BikersVote palm cards.

Just after sunset near the slaw pit, Dennis was taking my picture with one of the winners, who said to him, "Flash?" before he took the shot. "Yes," he replied, thinking she wanted to make sure the camera flash was on. It was not what she meant.

Driving around town, seeing all these tough-looking folks on incredible machines made you think, gee, you'd hate to be an enemy invading this country. The u.s. military is rather redundant. Yes, inside the head scarves and leathers are many lawyers and accountants on fantasy weekends, but even so, I'm sure if you announced to them that the North Koreans were invading Boca Raton, it would all be over by Miller Time.

■ ■ ■

We woke up on March 4, 2004, on an organic farm near Ocala, Florida, just south of Gainesville. Pauline Copello was misting her vegetables when I stumbled out of the house. Pauline's husband, Joel, and their four-year-old, Anthony, were busy with chores here and there. Pauline's parents, Beth and Tony Ehrlich, were indoors fixing us a farm breakfast. They had all sold their homes in Daytona and Ormond Beach a year and a half earlier to move to where Pauline could have land enough for her vegetables and where Beth and Tony could grow old. Joel does antique shows and Pauline has a delivery route for her organics. We talked about basil that morning—their most reliable cash crop. There are dozens of varieties, and some are so perishable you must eat them immediately upon picking.

Later in the morning, I was in a chair under a tree working on a speech. Dennis was working on the website. I looked around and thought that this is the kind of sustainable America that more of us need to get into. Urban versions, of course, will also be necessary. In the miles ahead, I would see many families and friends working it out, just like this family and the Hammonds back in Gettysburg.

It's not simple living. People say that's what we need, but sustainable living is not simple. Simple living is what the corporations would have us do: working late, coming home to a frozen dinner, watching the same shows on TV, having the same credit card debt. That's simple living. Life at its best is rich, beautiful, delicious, full of everything complex, colorful, and aromatic.

Living the life of democracy, and joyfully so, is the main thing the political progressives have to sell, in my opinion, and it has to be done by example. It is not about anger and screeching: joy attracts and energizes.

The Copello farm had indeed energized me, and we had miles to go that morning.

Dennis Kucinich was going to speak that evening in Gainesville, and I was to meet him there. I had been pressuring him and Howard Dean to join forces after the Democratic Convention, as the progressives were presently so split by the two campaigns. I wanted to get a promise out of Dennis K. before the Boston convention, and he had agreed to meet. We had met several times before.

Halfway to Gainesville, Rosie began sputtering, then absolutely died. She would need a full hour cool-down, and we didn't have time for that, or I would miss my meeting.

Blue and I stuck out our thumbs while Dennis fiddled with the engine. A woman in a red pickup truck stopped. She was planning to turn eastward to some other destination, but went many miles out of her way to get us to the meeting on time. Dennis and the vehicle arrived toward the end of the evening, with ice bags packed around her engine. Mr. Kucinich agreed to call Dean and get talks going about a joint event during the convention, which would in fact happen.

We drove on, back to Jacksonville, then west along the Florida Panhandle: the little stops along the way to cool down gave Blue a chance to dash into convenience markets and taverns and come out with a new voter or two. I liked how she was taking the lead on that more and more.

"Felon form!" she often said when she came out, and we would dig through the boxes for the right packet.

By this time we had stopped twenty times or more at repair garages. The mechanics of this great nation are nice fellows who look off into the distance to a special place when you describe an engine problem. It is a kind of meditation, a communion with all things mechanical. It is an entertainment to watch them think, especially when they brighten and raise their postures and ask an important question. But, no, we already had that replaced. Ahh. A grimace, then a moment of solemn acceptance, a tug on the grease-billed NAPA hat or the gray goatee and a return to the half-trance where the ultimate but ever-shrouded reality awaits the disciplined seeker. A head gasket, not yet replaced, was the most likely and least affordable guess many would make. A gap in the head gasket can send a jet of plasma-hot exhaust gasses into the engine compartment, where it can find a gasoline line or otherwise make dangerous trouble in a hurry. So we kept the two fire extinguishers under the front seats, and we kept the back door unlocked when we were under way.

One morning west of Jacksonville, while staying in the farm home of a carpenter, Mark Rothermel, who had read about us on the Internet and caught up with us on the streets of downtown Jacksonville, I went for a morning walk and got rather lost. A jogging woman with a cell phone saved the day. She dropped her jaw a bit later when Dennis and Blue drove up in the sparkling, alligator-ornamented, multicolored dream bus. "My ride," I said.

After Jacksonville, as we headed into warmer days, we stopped at a hardware store and Dennis bought about thirty feet of clear plastic tubing. He secured one end to the kitchen faucet in the back of the vehicle, and ran the tube through the cabin and out the window, along the hood, where Tim the Alligator held it in his teeth. From there, it dipped down to the front grille. The next time the engine started to stall and smoke, I was to run back and put a little water through the tube. The damn thing worked; the engine smoothed right out, and we kept going. It was not the first high-five of the adventure, but one of the most satisfying. The twenty-gallon water tank would get us down any road.

I was steaming along, too. Blue and Dennis kept an eye on my energy and general health. I had my low days, but not many. Blue provided muscle massages and used her magic oils and scents. I would nap on the narrow couch as we drove, sometimes waking with screams, as my legs would cramp up terribly. Blue would fix them again.

We had Mr. Springsteen's music on as we barreled toward Tallahassee. I was also developing a taste for Eminem, Dead Prez, and other groups. Blue liked spacey, New Age music that put me right to sleep. I liked the rap music because I had a little rap routine I had used in clubs in college towns, and it was quite a hit. But I had a lot to learn.

The home of Susie Caplowe and Dan Hendrickson in Tallahassee is very nice and quite what you might expect of a normal American home until you open the door from the laundry room into what used to be a two-car garage. Computers, voting precinct maps, file cabinets, and bins of clippings, reports, and plans stretch out before you. I'm sure Karl Rove doesn't even have such a garage. Susie and Dan, an important part of the Florida progressive and environmental community, took us in, briefed us on the blow-by-blow of the 2000 debacle, which they had witnessed, and set us up with events and press interviews.

For Susie and Dan, the men who came in from Washington to physically stop the vote counting through belly-bouncing intimidation was a white-hot memory, and it was fueling their voter work now.

Over the next few days, we created two television stories, a newspaper story, and a public radio story that ran statewide. Another ran nationally on NPR. Gayle White of the *Atlanta Journal-Constitution* was traveling with us and wrote a fine story. We worked outside grocery stores in African American neighborhoods with the volunteers Susie recruited. The evenings were rallies and coordination meetings with voting rights and voter awareness groups, some of which Susie had started.

We finally connected with NOW and even met the state chair of the ghostly Florida Democratic Party. He would only talk to us if we walked with him from a podium to his car. We pitched him on what we had been doing in Florida and what the party could do to follow up, especially in regard to housing projects and churches. His flunky gave me a card but never returned our calls. It was sort of the perfect last experience with the Democratic Party in Florida. You could tell they were pulling out all the stops to lose another one for America.

I went to a meeting of the North Florida Democratic Club one evening. They had lovely cookies. They look confused and a little disturbed when we mentioned that we had been through their low-income neighborhoods and everyone we signed up to vote claimed to have never seen anyone from the Democratic Party in their neighborhoods before. They were happy for the next speaker.

We felt better after a big union barbecue at the fairgrounds and a student march on the Capitol.

Before we left town, Blue, I am told, gave Susie a little tattoo somewhere.

■ ■ ■

Paulette, our hostess in New Orleans, a poet and literature professor at Loyola of New Orleans, is a refined but tough, good-looking woman. She had long ago shared a drink or two with Tennessee Williams. She still occasionally drank at Molly's in the Quarter with poet Andrei Codrescu. She took us to the shipyards and ferry stations where people might need to register, and helped us register all along

Canal Street. She set me up as guest bartender at Molly's, where I got on a first-name basis with the many reporters who call the place home.

We set up our voter registration tables in the Ninth Ward and in other rough areas, and did a very good business. We were welcomed so warmly everywhere that we didn't want to leave.

Paulette and her son, David, were Rock the Vote organizers, which connected us with several voter projects in the city, and with the up-start League of Independent Voters, also known at that time as the League of Pissed-Off Voters, which Blue rather liked. She made some friends and collected emails from the group. We offered some exper-tise on ex-felon voting that the local groups needed—they had been operating under false information and had been turning away many people who could in fact register.

A very Republican family who lived across the road from Paulette—right under the levee, in fact—stopped when they saw Blue painting on the back of the vehicle one morning and just had to know all about our adventure. They invited us to dinner, which was a one-act southern play of accents and attitudes, family generational stresses, and conver-sations in the garden of their fine home.

The next night, our intended departure night, they invited us up to their friend's apartment in the Quarter, a luxurious place where we overlooked lively Bourbon Street from an iron balcony—as the ladies kept filling our glasses. They were lovely, well-informed people, and were particularly concerned about the loss of wetlands protecting New Orleans. Eleven football fields' worth of wetlands were lost each year. The wetlands are the city's only shield from hurricanes.

The ladies were also concerned about the mess in Iraq, and we seemed to have many other shared concerns. I suppose our failure to understand how they could get from those concerns to a support for Mr. Bush was as mysterious to us as our connection of dots was myste-rious to them. But, like most American voters, what they seemed to like most were people who were authentic, who understood what they believed and took action. It made us fit company for them that night. Parties and candidates were inconsequential when put next to good character and good whiskey.

Poor Blue, whose southern soul seemed so at home on that balcony, could not breathe; the early spring pollen was a thick blanket upon the city. Even in her excitement to discover more voodoo shops and talk with interesting people, even in her ecstatic gyrations down jazz-filled streets—she took me to visit and photograph graveyards and crypts late one night—even in her blissful pose at Molly's and at sidewalk cafés where she visited compatriots of her age and artistic bent, even in all this joy, she could not get a proper breath of air. We simply had to leave.

These memories of course hit me hard after the hurricane of 2005. Paulette, after the storm, resigned her post at Loyola so that younger faculty members with families could keep their jobs. She moved to New York where her daughter lives. The ladies of the great house and the balcony survived, though they know some who did not. Their house by the levee was ravaged but not destroyed. They are among those who have come back with great moral courage to rebuild and to help others rebuild.

15

FROM THE VERY BALCONY

*W*e roared up Louisiana and into Mississippi, stopping at dawn for breakfast and a few loads of laundry. We finally found signs of a Democratic Party: a laundry attendant in Canton could give us a good report on party organizing and registration in the area.

We sat in the laundry and waited for our clothes to stop spinning. In the first miles of the trip we would each run our own loads. Then, maybe somewhere in Miami, it was a ladies' load and a gents' load. Now, to save quarters and because we were pretty much family, a mixed load was acceptable.

Waiting in launderettes and elsewhere, I liked to read advance copies of books from Jim Hightower and Molly Ivins, who never fail to make me laugh. Blue would have her music in her earphones and would be reading something more spiritual or mythological. Dennis would be emailing people ahead.

We had a date in Memphis with the Hip Hop Summit Voter Project, which was backed by a big rap promoter, Russell Simmons. Also, I had been invited as the main speaker for the thirty-fifth commemoration of Dr. King's death in Memphis. I would speak from the Lorraine Motel balcony where he was killed. The idea did not seem real to me. It was too much of an honor. I didn't know if I could do it without breaking down.

We hit the blues joints on Beale Street within minutes of our arrival in Memphis. The next day we registered voters in the housing projects along Vance Boulevard. The children of the projects, like those in so many other places, were mesmerized by Tim the Alligator and by Rosie generally. I expect Tim had been petted now by a few hundred kids, each saying at least "Whoa!" as they did so, and some carrying on great conversations: "What you doin' to my finger, Tim? You gonna eat my finger, Tim? Looks like you been eatin' bugs, Tim. You like them bugs? You gotta brush your teeth, Tim."

The day arrived. We went to the Lorraine Motel, now called the National Civil Rights Museum. The courtyard was filled with hundreds of people, many in their teens and nearly all African American by descent.

"My God, I'm I going to speak from there?" I looked up at the place where King was shot, a wreath on the railing to mark the spot. "That's sacred; I don't know if I can do it." Dennis reminded me I had spoken from the steps of the Lincoln Memorial and the U.S. Capitol, and had not lost my composure.

Reverend Lennox Yearwood Jr. and a young man helped me up the stairway. I looked out at the crowd, over to the wreath, then across the way to the fire department headquarters where the shooter may have stood and done so much harm to us all. The crowd grew still and quiet. The words came very naturally to me in that moment:

Before many of you were born, but only yesterday evening to me, a shot rang out through this air, among these buildings, that rocked our culture, advanced a wave of despair and violence, ended a great life, interrupted the effort to end the injustice of poverty in America. The years have passed. The violence is now different, but it is still here. The despair is different, but it saturates us and sometimes immobilizes us. The great moral imperative of ending poverty in America seems far away, for many in power now do everything they can to widen, not narrow, the gap between rich and poor.

The people began to respond with "that's right" and "yes."

The dark forces that brought death to this doorstep — America's doorstep — and that ended the lives of our other great leaders, are still with us, doing what they do to keep us from being the masters of our own government, of our own futures, keeping us from making our government and our society clear reflections and instruments of our own highest values. We live now in a commercialized culture that tries every day and in a thousand ways to assassinate our moral sensibilities. But we are strong, and even my old eyes can still see injustice clearly, and even my old heart can feel the presence and guidance of the great soul who was transformed, but hardly killed, on this very spot.

It is up to us to be awake, and to embrace the joy of life and of the good community, no mater what. It is up to us to set examples, to project our values and vision for a better world, no matter what. It is up to us to use the institutions of our democracy, damaged and struggling though they are, to move our people forward again from a troubled time, no matter what.

The crowd was now repeating after me and reacting to each thought. I had no more fear at all.

America has a quiet revolution every four years. We find ourselves at a critical time in our nation's history. We call upon the spirits of these great souls who gave their lives to us with such love and wisdom. Yes, Dr. King, we understand that our sacrifice brings forth victory for the truth if we will but sacrifice enough. Yes, Dr. King, we will awaken every citizen we can. We will register them to vote, and take them by the hand on voting day.

I am on a long trek to make a small sacrifice of my own, to show that, at my age and infirmity, if I can go to distant cities to register voters, certainly others can take time and energy to do it in their home towns, college campuses, housing projects, and neighborhoods. We must not be afraid to be out there, saying what must be said, and doing what democracy needs of us now. Dr. King reminds us to spend our lives generously in the cause of love.

Young people were perched in the trees, waving their arms and calling back to me as I spoke.

Love is more powerful than violence. It is cleansing and liberating and energizing and joyful. Love washes away despair and fear. Love is freedom, and freedom is love. By the simple act of declaring our love and respect for one another, we are on the mountain King could see. All violence is down below us. All injustice is down below us. It nips at our heels, but we do not stop walking, we do not stop climbing. Dr. King and so many other great souls still walk with us, climb with us, every day, every night, every moment that we embrace our lives as our own, embrace our nation as our own, embrace each other as our brothers and sisters in the great community we are ever building, no matter what.

I was helped down the steps, and I made good contacts in the crowd for the road ahead.

From there, it was housing projects in St. Louis. By the time we reached Des Moines, Dean had screamed his scream and was gone—the progressives were still in mourning. Kerry was sailing to the convention in Dean's place.

In the first miles of Minnesota, approaching Mankato, a fierce storm about blew Rosie apart—a semi truck tipped over as we watched. Rosie was rocking dangerously as dry cornstalks swirled thick in the wind and turned chain-link fences into solid walls, which then bent over in the gale. A tornado warning came over the radio, and dark purple swirls tumbled down from the greenish clouds above.

Nick Palumbo, a great organizer and good friend from this part of the world, was at the wheel. He fought to get Rosie away from the storm, but a fierce headwind was overheating the engine, and there was no time for the old cooling tricks. We dashed into a gas station, flew out of Rosie, and huddled with other travelers in the station office.

The power went off as the outside turned a sickly green. Visibility fell to zero as the whole station rocked and bits of everything thumped and cracked against the windows. When the worst of it passed, Rosie was still there, still shaking a bit like everyone else. We got back in and Nick fought the headwind down the road—overheating and stalling a dozen times as we tried to get to Mankato in time for my speech. A delegation of townspeople finally came out to fetch me in a fast car.

In Minneapolis, Nick lived in a big house with three pretty women college students. It was a cooperative housing situation, with everybody doing a share of chores and cooking.

Nick was currently working with a Minnesota reform group that was pushing public campaign financing, and we had agreed to be useful in getting press and campus attention. We would combine that message with a voter registration push across the state, two colleges a day, all the way up to the blue ice of Duluth. I led marches with mayors and hundreds of students. Retirees were mixing into the crowds. It was a glimpse of the great joining of generations that we had been hoping might come to pass: the '60s peaceniks with the new generation of students. They could be an unstoppable force if they came together nationally, as would happen later in the Obama campaign.

It was the middle of April, and we had been on the road for over six months. Every place had been different enough that every day seemed new and energizing. Blue was getting to know midwesterners. I believe she was inspired by their earnest sincerity and, well, niceness. Her daily exposure to students was making her think about where she might fit into all that. She had attended college in North Carolina, but problems intervened. I knew how that felt.

We were doing all right in Minnesota—front page news and all over TV, generating lots of new energy for the public financing of campaigns. Nick was flying high as his bill picked up cosponsors. Voter registration? It just isn't a problem in Minnesota, as they actually want people to vote in that state and make it easy. You just go vote. You don't need a passport, a letter of transit, or a note from the principal. You can register at the polls on Election Day. But we were still getting out the message that working women must vote.

Minneapolis has a perfect-picture spot where you can talk about working women. It's a statue on Nicollet Avenue—a pedestrian and trolley street—where a bronze Mary Tyler Moore statue tosses up her bronze beret. We ended the week there, then headed to Wisconsin, our twentieth state. Madison is the home of American progressive reform, and I had always wanted to see the streets once walked by Fighting Bob La Follette, the man behind every reform Teddy Roosevelt took credit for. It's the region where farms and Main Street rebelled against big banks, big railroad, and corrupt politics. With his cohort, university president Charles Van Hise, Governor La Follette turned Madison into a kind of citywide think tank. By engaging the experts at the University of Wisconsin and the state government in a problem-solving co-op, most of what we know as progressive reform politics was hatched. The direct election of U.S. senators, the workers' compensation system, citizen ballot initiatives, and many other reforms came out of that happy arrangement, which continues today.

We did our thing in Madison—the media stories, walks, voter events, meeting great people—and moved on. Now flying without the precision of Nick's minute-by-minute planning, we felt a bit slipshod. But Wisconsin was another free move—a just-go-vote state like Minnesota. Anyway, there was a super organizer waiting for us just ahead in Chicago.

And, yes, I was getting as exhausted as you must be by now.

FINDING LIFE EVERYWHERE

16

*T*he concrete stairwells of Cabrini-Green in Chicago were stained with bloody handprints. Blue was appalled but fascinated. She took pictures of the unintended art. Steel shutters secured every window, and the big, brown eyes of little children often peeked through the slits when we knocked—and we knocked on every door. Prisons are much nicer places. Many of the apartment interiors, however, were clean and lively, and many of the children were nicely dressed and courteous. Because of its reputation for being the most violent housing project in America, most of the towers have been taken down; only a few remain, and they stare down on empty parking lots—few residents can afford cars. Rosie was about the only vehicle in the lot, far down below us, as we worked the buildings.

"Would you like to register to vote? On Election Day, you can vote right across the parking lot at the school."

The door would open wider. "Yes, please. How do I do it?"

Most people claimed to have never met anyone doing voter work in the buildings. We were as welcome as if we were handing out chocolate and silver dollars.

We traveled in groups, registering people on almost every floor.

Certainly one of the most amazing organizers in the country was with us, plus volunteers she had recruited for us.

Andrea Raila, a tax consultant, had followed my big walk and our recent travels via the Internet and had promised to have Chicago ready for us, which she did. Andrea moved us through Cabrini with a forceful spirit. Our clipboards started filling up. Another volunteer, Raj, who registered with us, said he would organize more volunteers to do the other buildings and to do the get-out-the-vote effort.

When we were resting downstairs before we left, a young man gave us the social history of Cabrini. Before all the housing cutbacks of the Bush administration, people from the wider community used to come around more often. They would bring school supplies and clothing for the kids. But that had taken some coordination and staffing, which the housing department no longer enjoyed. Now the residents are very much alone, feeling abandoned by the community and separated from its promises and values. Many residents work at jobs, but minimum wage can't get them out of the projects. Criminal records, acquired in youth, keep many of them down and out.

I found myself crying from time to time on this trip, mostly from trying to get through Jonathan Kozol's book about the education system and the poor. Here it all was, all around us—its urine- and blood-soaked stairs and its desperation, and yet its clean and well-spoken kids who deserved so much better. Cabrini is the place where a young boy was dangled from his heels and dropped to his death for refusing to sell drugs. The reality of being there overwhelmed me. That night, particularly, it really hit me very hard. I needed to be consoled by my friends.

■ ■ ■

Ben Cohen, my ice cream friend of Ben & Jerry's, uses cookies to make a point about how lobbyists distort the way our tax dollars are spent. If each cookie represents ten billion dollars, the Pentagon gets forty cookies; schools get three and a half; world hunger gets one; alternative energy gets one-fourth; children's health gets four. If you took five cookies from the Pentagon, we would still have double the military budget of all other countries combined, and we could provide food for all the children of the world. We could also end U.S. childhood poverty, rebuild our schools, and so on. Anyway, that's why I was crying, because with all our work and protests and letters and walks and election work, we are still five cookies short of a decent society.

The next day we covered the LeClaire housing projects with a *Tribune* reporter in tow. Andrea was again our organizer, using the red wagon to pull her two younger kids down the streets. We also spent a day with her downtown under the el, registering students at Harold Washington College.

Andrea and her husband, Michael, had adopted a child from China. When the little girl became sad one night that there was nobody else in the family quite like her, Andrea and Mike said, OK, let's go to China and get you a sister, and they did. There seems to be no sadness in the world that they will not happily jump into to make right. Andrea is white, but a black woman had helped raise her. The woman, Elmira, had a son who was killed by the KKK during the civil rights struggle. To Andrea, it was like the loss of a brother.

It was spring, and the flower boxes down the middle of Michigan Avenue were gorgeous. Chicago is a beautiful town, Cabrini and all. The sun on the lake makes the whole city sparkle and breathe deeply. We registered voters on State Street, that great street; we hoisted the Polish flag from old Rosie in the Polish Day Parade.

Then it was on to Detroit.

We pulled into a metered parking spot on Nine Mile Road in Ferndale, a town within the Detroit metropolis. We had contacts in Detroit for the days ahead, but not for this night, getting in so late. We had taken extra time in Battle Creek when we discovered Sojourner Truth's grave there. It somehow seemed like a place we had to stop and pay respects.

So that first night near Detroit was one of those nights with Blue sleeping up in the loft, as my legs were still cramping; I was on the narrow bench seat, and Dennis was on the narrower floor. You worry about that in Detroit—sleeping parked on the street like that.

There was a bang on the front window in early dawn. I was sure we were being rousted out by either a gang or by the constabulary. No, it was the city manager of Ferndale, with a tray of hot coffees. The folks at the Greenhouse, a progressive activist center just upstairs from our parking place, had spotted us and notified friends in City Hall. It was going to be like that. The city manager told us that the parking meters were not for us to worry about, and to save our quarters—the meter maid had been so advised. He invited me to come to the city council meeting that evening and receive a key to the city. To tell you the truth, I cannot get enough of those things—they are so pretty.

We were given an office in the Greenhouse, where activists were at the time working on instant runoff voting as their next reform. That is where you rank your choice of candidates, a much more sensible way to vote than primaries and generals and runoffs. They would later win that reform. They also were about to launch a community radio station, but without the required FCC permit. The reason for that was the Bush administration had let organizations like Clear Channel buy up all available licenses. The interesting thing about this pirate station was that its backers included the mayor and some council members — a modest revolution.

We quickly connected with Kathy Gauthier and her mother, Irene, who ran a health and therapeutic massage center in a big new building. This was exactly the medicine I needed. By day we combed the housing projects of Detroit, and by night Kathy and Irene rebuilt me, head to toe.

Blue discovered colored chalk and invested in a big bucketful. In the housing projects, she would write her name in big, stylized letters on the sidewalk. There would soon be a dozen or more children writing their names and drawing butterflies and a thousand other things. The mothers would come to see the transformation spreading over the walkways of the projects. Then our clipboards would come out.

By asking a lot of questions, we identified the natural leaders of each housing project and tried to connect them with volunteers who would stay in touch and help them host Election Day barbecue parties for voters.

Highland Park, near central Detroit, was until recently the home of Chrysler Corporation and other auto giants. It was the first home of Ford's Model T plant. Chrysler had recently pulled out, leaving the town high and dry — it couldn't afford to fix the potholes on its streets, which were like the moon.

Into this corporation-created mess now rode the corporations to steal a profit: the world's largest water company was bidding to privatize the community's water supply. The financial affairs of the city had been turned over to a pro-privatization executor, appointed by the previous Republican governor. The executor, who was given the undemocratic power to overrule the actions of the mayor and council, was paid enough money to pave quite a few streets: a quarter million a year. The people were being taken for a shakedown ride on their own bumpy streets.

In Highland Park, it seemed clear that the industrial era was over and a lack of political imagination was retarding a rebirth. It was obvious that they needed to focus on keeping their money in local circulation until they invented something better. You can have a prosperous community just with local stores and local production for local needs, but there seemed no leadership for anything but anger. I spoke up a little about it.

Detroit still bears the scars of the 1960s, when riots raged and white families moved out. Eight Mile Road was, and still is, the racial dividing line. We had heard a rumor that there was actually an eight-mile wall, a Berlin Wall, still standing. Officials of Detroit told us there was no such thing, but we found it. It was built to divide a white subdivision from a property owned by an African American family. The wall wasn't the fault of the people of Detroit, but was mandated by the Federal Housing Administration right after World War II. FHA wouldn't guarantee loans in racially mixed areas, so the wall went up to show the white area was separate. The gray stucco wall was standing in the rain when we found it: "8 Mile" had been spray-painted on it by someone who obviously didn't want that history forgotten. City Hall certainly wasn't going to put a plaque on it.

On the way out of Detroit we went across the water to Windsor, Ontario, to get a breath of Canadian air. I had asked someone in Detroit if we needed passports, and they assured us that people run across for lunch or dinner all the time.

Dennis and I had nothing but our driver's licenses. Blue had her passport. We had some explaining to do to get back into the United States. Our subversive vehicle was the problem. We were ushered into the security building through a door marked "personal search" and were turned over to a young man in uniform. Sternly, he asked us all about our journey. He disappeared for quite a long time into a back room. I finally saw him coming toward us down the hall, a serious look on his mug. "Nice website," he said. He walked us out to Rosie and asked how he could become more involved. He gave us his email address and sent us on our way.

We had Ohio, a critical state, yet ahead, but everyone was exhausted. Blue suggested we take a break in Asheville. It would give us time to do a proper job of organizing Ohio. I agreed. Besides, we had been getting on each other's nerves. We needed to slow down for a few days.

We were invited to Heartwood, a Forest Council conference not far from Asheville. The activist retreat in the deep woods sounded like a good place to recharge. Actor Woody Harrelson had invited me; I rather liked him when we met a year earlier at the same event. He had given me something to smoke, by the way, that made me giggle. He shotgunned it, as they say. It happened in a bus full of young people, who cheered. I figured that, if in my political days to come, some reporter or official might ask me if I had ever used marijuana, I would say, yes, indeed, but I had not inhaled. Oh really? Yes, truly, I would reply. I would say that I didn't need to inhale because Woody Harrelson had shotgunned a huge load of it right into my lungs from his. Then I would watch the reaction. The fact is, I did feel a little guilty about it. I hadn't felt so felonious since drinking gin during Prohibition.

Once we had settled into Rebecca MacNeice's Asheville home again, Blue took us up into the Smokies, where we walked though the great beauty of the mountains. We soaked under a small waterfall in a secret place of hers, keeping most of our clothes on. Just sitting in that beauty together, far from the things of man, I think we three finally felt completely like pals again.

Blue showed us her Asheville, and her old haunts. Her long walks to and from downtown had taken her under the Patton Avenue Bridge, where there were some rough neighborhoods and homeless camps along the railroad lines and the French Broad River. The river is trimmed in grapevine, Christmas ferns, laurel, bittersweet, and a garden of medicinal plants that were part of Blue's botanica: maidenhair fern, wild ginger, butterfly weed, wild indigo, witch hazel, Indian tobacco, red raspberry, elderberry, wood nettle, hawthorn, bloodroot, sassafras, yellow root, wild yam, striped gentian, hepatica, goldenrod, and a thousand other things one might use to soothe or cure or beautify.

She explained how the French Broad flows between the Great Smokies and the Blue Ridge and has made Asheville a whitewater adventure center. Indeed, kayaks hang from the ceilings of beer bars, and a young, outdoorsy confidence energizes the town. That athletic energy mixes with the more nocturnal world of artists, political progressives, and revolutionaries, all on their various paths. Blue had a sense of the big picture of it.

Asheville is an old brick town built on a spruce and pine hill, the dome of which introduces enough curves to the streets to make the town interesting. The campus of UNC Asheville, up in the woods on the north end, makes Asheville politically progressive and cosmopolitan, though that necessarily makes it an outpost under siege in a conservative landscape.

Greenery and money insinuate the town. The Vanderbilt family built their great mansion, Biltmore, on the south end of town. To plan Biltmore's gardens, the Vanderbilts brought in Frederick Law Olmstead, whose other credits include the Boston Public Garden, New York's Central Park, and San Francisco's Golden Gate Park. Biltmore remains the largest privately owned home in America, with an entry that is more scenic highway than driveway. Other fortunes have built other homes in Asheville, though the town has gently absorbed big money without succumbing to snobbery or lining its streets with the kind of stores that follow newer money.

On our way out of North Carolina, heading toward the forest conference, we stopped at Blue's grandparents' home. Its big screen porch looks over a meadow. Two of her uncles got out their guitars and played and sang. I don't think they hardly recognized Blue: she was a confident, respected organizer now, taking cell phone calls from important people. It was great to let her family see her in this new light. They had always known that she was special — "an exotic flower," her grandmother told me — but they didn't know she was also going to do such things in the world. She had already seen far more of it than they had. Blue was feeling the difference, too. She had received an email that day from a noted activist leader, asking for political advice and comparing notes for the campaign season ahead. Blue was coming into focus.

After a few days at the Forest Council conference deep in the Shenandoah Valley, we headed back to New England. Blue split off with Marlo Poras, a filmmaker who had traveled with us off and on since Chicago, to go see New York City for the first time. She fell in love with the place, of course. She would catch a ride north to New Hampshire a few days later.

Dennis would go back to Arizona for a week to see his Maureen. But first he would drive me home to New Hampshire. It was June 4, 2004. We had logged twenty-three thousand miles and had done business in all the swing states east of the Mississippi except Ohio. The plan was to relax for a week, restock, and head for the western swing states, stopping in Ohio for two weeks.

I was coughing badly, so Dennis said we might need to give me more rest time. He was worried about me, I believe. I was ninety-four, which is reason enough, of course. It was wonderful to get back to my big bathtub and my good books and a real kitchen and all my friends.

That's when things took a wild turn.

THE WIND SHIFTS

17

*T*wo days later, Dennis was home in Phoenix when Jim and I called him with the news.

"Mom's thinking about running for the U.S. Senate," Jim said. "If so, she has the Democratic nomination in the bag. The party will back her."

New Hampshire's Democratic candidate for the U.S. Senate had dropped out because his campaign manager absconded with all the funds. The party needed someone to run against Judd Gregg, the immensely popular incumbent, and nobody had the nerve to do it at this last minute.

When I got on the line, Dennis told me I suddenly sounded ten years younger, which would be eighty-four. He said it would be much tougher than the voter trek, as people would be gunning for me, trying to trip me up, and digging for family skeletons. I wouldn't get the sweet grandma treatment. The swift-boat thing had happened just a month earlier to smear Kerry's war record.

A ninety-four-year-old candidate running for a six-year term in the U.S. Senate? Could we sell the idea of a centenarian in the Senate? Dennis wasn't so sure it was a good idea.

Jim told him I couldn't win, and that wasn't the point, which was right. "She can talk about campaign finance reform and Bush. Gregg will run unopposed otherwise. We can pin him down and maybe swing New Hampshire to Kerry," he said.

Dennis was on a plane the next morning.

The woman executive director of the New Hampshire Democratic Party took Jim and me aside on the day I became the party's candidate. She said she wanted an assurance that I would support the party's candidate for president. I was floored that she would ask.

She said she was asking because of a speech or statement I had made years earlier encouraging people to vote their hearts, that even a vote for a candidate who could not win would build a constituency for later change. The Nader people had circulated the statement, and this woman believed it might have helped divide the New Hampshire vote. If Mr. Bush had not won New Hampshire in 2000, he would not have taken the election as easily.

It was a speech of another era, before all the unimaginable damage of the Bush administration. In that earlier era, we wondered if there was really a difference between the parties, both so bought and sold. There was, in fact, a remarkable difference.

"My God," I said to Jim on the way home, "am I responsible for every horror of the last four years?"

We looked up the numbers: Gore lost New Hampshire by seven thousand votes. Nader had over twenty-two thousand votes. Had, say, a third of Nader's votes come to him because of my speech? That was simply not possible. Ten percent at the outside, probably half of that. But it was something to worry about as I tried to sleep that night. I hadn't caused the Great Depression either, but there is always a nightmare part of you that blames and worries. It is true that the changes we bring forth as activists are never fully under our control. That is a warning to be thoughtful, not to disengage.

When I was a young mother I organized a sleigh ride for town children. One little girl was severely injured when she tried to jump on the moving sleigh. That has haunted me, and so I have tried to be thoughtful and careful. Even so, things happen when you take action in the world, and you must accept the fact that sometimes you will do unintended harm. You still must take your part. Friendly fire is what it is called in other parts. It happens.

There is a story in the Bhagavad Gita, in which the warrior Arjuna, on a hill with Lord Krishna, hesitates to start the battle because he will be killing some of his own kin. Krishna, in essence, says, hey, nobody really dies, and you have a job to do. You are an imperfect soldier in the great struggle between light and dark. Do your duty.

By the time Dennis returned from Arizona, Blue had already rounded up lists of New England volunteers. Jim was on the phone to the party headquarters in Concord—conversations that rarely went well.

I made a public statement that the campaign would not accept donations from political action committees, only from individuals. That pretty much sealed the fact that it was going to be a symbolic campaign. Given my long fight against big money in politics, it was the right thing to say, but it hurt to think about all the money we were not going to get. We would have to run on dimes instead of dollars, but we knew how to do that.

My living room filled with used computers and telephones. A satellite dish was installed on the roof. The conversation pit at the far end, near the fireplace, filled with sleeping bags and file cabinets. With tents and cots we set up a volunteer camp on the bluff across the creek, building a little bridge over the water out of junk wood from the dump. We scouted Manchester and Concord for a headquarters office, unsure if we really needed that. Maybe an office down the hill in Peterborough would be enough, which is what we finally decided.

From my announcement at the state Capitol:

I make my pledge right now to stick to one term, and I have the biological ability to follow through with that pledge, while Mr. Gregg, who two elections ago made a pledge to not run for a third term, has neither the ripe age nor, it seems, the willpower to deliver on his promise.

The press corps was enjoying the fun. They could sense that this would be an interesting race to cover.

For those who may doubt my capacity to serve, let me assure them that, while I may struggle for the right word from time to time, I can yet string my words together somewhat better than even our current president. And, while I need glasses for some reading, I can see clearly the difference between a necessary war and an unnecessary war, and the difference between a balanced budget and a deficit. Most importantly, I can read the Constitution and its Bill of Rights very easily and clearly, and, when elected, I will do what so many others in today's Washington have not had the decency to do, and that is to abide by their oath to defend it.

I am running for the U.S. Senate against a good man, Judd Gregg, who has allowed himself to become an enabler of George Bush and his neo-con scourge now afflicting our nation and the world. I, Doris Haddock, am running so that our voters might at the very least send Mr. Gregg a message: that we expect our senators to represent common sense and the interests of our country and of our working people and children, even when to do so requires the courage to go against one's party. And I am running to do a favor for my many Republican friends who are most uncomfortable with how far their once-venerable party has strayed—once a bastion of sensible federal spending and small business defense.

■ ■ ■

I began taking longer walks each morning to limber up for the campaign trail. Though Dublin is far from any city or freeway, reporters from as far as Japan walked with me down to Karr's Market or to the Dublin General Store for a *New York Times* and a collection of New Hampshire papers. My wheezing and coughing were a continuing threat to the enterprise. Sometimes I would just have to rest before answering a reporter's question. We would sit together on a log.

We immediately found political experts in key issue areas who would come up to Dublin and help us lay out important positions: the economy, terror, Iraq, veterans, health—all of it. It was time for realism and accuracy. Some of the experts took up residency in the camp across the creek for a few days or a week while they did their work, wrote their summaries, and briefed me: Fran from Tallahassee; Kathleen from Washington—an expert who worked with congressional committees; David from Boston, who was a top Pentagon consultant on defense and veterans' issues. His wife, also a wizard planner and researcher, practiced her violin in the living room. The porch deck and the kitchen and the big living room became a beehive of volunteers, with accompaniment.

We began the search for a campaign manager, as Jim and Dennis could not see themselves doing that. It was late in the campaign season, and most of the good people were already engaged. But after the Democratic Convention in Boston there would undoubtedly be some good people up for grabs, as all but one of the presidential campaigns would have folded. We made plans to attend.

Right in Peterborough, a few miles from my home in Dublin, lived an ideal press secretary. She was a public relations professional, experienced in politics, and she instinctively understood my approach.

Maude Salinger was the niece of Pierre Salinger, who had been JFK's press secretary. She agreed to help.

Because we would never have much money for advertising, I needed to generate a flood of town-by-town coverage, and that meant walking the state. A neighbor up the hill, a gentleman of some local fame and of elegant dress and manner, brought some maps of New Hampshire's historic postal roads. They were still maintained as two-lane roads and looped through hundreds of towns and in and out of the major cities. That would give us multiple hits with the state's few television and daily newspapers.

I walked in local "town day" parades that pepper New Hampshire each spring. The day before the first one, in the picturesque town of Wilton, Jim was up at the community-supported farm, gathering food for our troops, when Leslie, a fellow co-op member, asked if I needed a band to march behind me in the parade. Fred and Leslie and their musician friends, called Tattoo, would be with me for the rest of the campaign: Fred on the trombone, Leslie on accordion, and friends with drums, trumpets, and tuba. They took "Just a Closer Walk with Thee," cranked it up to Dixieland, added new lyrics, and "Just a Walk with Granny D" started rocking the main streets and town squares of New Hampshire. With the town day parades, the campaign was off to a cheering start. Even Republicans with Bush buttons stood up along the parades to applaud or to rush out and shake hands.

From the north woods to the Massachusetts border, from the Portsmouth seacoast to the edge of Vermont, and from great spots like Robert Frost's front porch, I started telling it like it was, offering up what I hoped was a more visionary brand of politics than had been seen in awhile.

I don't mean that I never took a shot at my opponent, but I tried to keep things elevated. So did he. Our campaigns were unlike what was going on elsewhere, as America had already fallen into extreme politics.

Part of that was the result of the cultural stresses: the middle class, which is the foundation of democracy, was under great strain. The elites of both political parties had been shipping our best jobs overseas for more than a decade. And even in good times, it is true that as people grow older, it is difficult for them to not become more extreme in their politics. It is difficult to not be washed hard to the right or left by the flood of information that is edited by the tilt of our own (once slight) inclinations. The incline of our inclinations grows steeper with the years, unless checked by our own common sense or by healthy, fact-based news organizations—now nearly extinct. The balanced view, of course, is wisdom. But there is enough information in the world to conclusively prove or disprove any proposition, political or otherwise. The trick, then, is to filter this flood of information not through political ideologies, but through a deep love of people, including oneself.

Harsh political views are often not what people truly believe; they have adopted them not for their compelling logic, but for their psychological utility. Harsh views are often compensations for what our subconscious mind calculates to be missing in the world, thinking we are the usual case. So, if we see ourselves as selfish, too individualistic, the compensation will come in our politics and we will vote and argue for more kindness and cooperation and community in the world. And if, on the other hand, our subconscious calculates that we are too kindly and compliant, our outward politics can be downright mean and tight-fisted. The proof of this is all around: I will bet you that your warmest neighbors are your Republican neighbors, for example. As for us Democrats, someone once told me that if you want a lovely day with good people, join a gun club. But if you want downright hand-to-hand combat, get on the board of a peace group. You see how it works. So the best road to sensible, moderate, problem-solving politics—and peace—is to work on ourselves as we work on the world.

Be involved and fight the good fights, but remember, if it doesn't make you happy, it probably isn't good politics—it's you simply using the world for your own therapy. Work for what you believe, but do it with kindness and from love, rejecting the snake oils that keep people angry and divided. I've made some tough speeches against some politicians I thought were taking us down wrong roads. The meaner the speech, the less good it ever did. When I made speeches to energize people to do the right thing out of love, those words often made a difference.

In the campaign, we had to remind ourselves of that every day, which we did.

SHARED COURAGE

18

*O*ur relationship with the state party was rocky. They didn't take me seriously as a candidate, even as we started to attract big news stories. I was by rights the head of the New Hampshire delegation to the Democratic National Convention in Boston, being the candidate for the highest office, yet the party didn't even invite me to come as a part of the delegation. It was the old populist/elite split, I suppose. My age, of course, made me something of a sideshow in some eyes.

We went to the convention anyway and crashed the party. I only wish we had taken the band.

We actually went to Boston for a good reason: to recruit staff and advisers. I somehow got an invitation to the Bloggers' Ball and there had a drink with Joe Trippi. Blue went on a charm offensive with Joe: Yes, he might be willing to share some advice. Yes, we could list him as a campaign adviser. Finally, yes, he would come up to New Hampshire.

Nicco Melle, a superstar of political website engineering and the man, like Trippi, behind the web success of the Dean campaign, also agreed to help. It was a good evening.

The Dean rank-and-file were quickly hired up by the Kerry people. The Kucinich people, poor dears, were entirely available. We hired a few.

The big joint gathering of Kucinich and Dean volunteers that I had encouraged months earlier—that Blue and I had hitchhiked to promote back in Gainesville—actually happened as a side event of the Democratic Convention.

This is what I said from that podium:

There are so many things that I do not have to say to the people in this room. I do not have to go on and on about the danger our democracy faces right now. I do not have to lay out the case for the Bill of Rights or the environment or fair trade or world peace. I do not have to reason with you as to the case against torture or dictatorship. I do not have to speak to you about how we must not split our vote this year. I don't like preaching to the faithful, so let me tell you something you may not have thought about.

Our present emergency is upon us because our civic society has been dumbed down by dumbed-down newspapers, radio, and television news, by dumbed-down schools, and by a corporate-run economic rat race that keeps people so busy trying to make ends meet that they have no time nor energy left for the civic affairs of their town or nation. You certainly know all this, and we celebrate the rise of independent media and the use of books and films to fill in some of the gaps. But the gaps are awesome, and democracy cannot long survive when the people are not well informed, interested, and supplied with sufficient time and resources to participate.

But there is another thing that has been dumbed down over the past two or three generations, and that is the art of politics itself.

If the politics of a century ago can be likened to a banquet, the politics of today is like a fast-food burger.

I am going to try to sell you on the idea of a richer politics, so let me tell you what it used to be like. Everybody used to be involved. You went to your Elks Club or your Women's Club, but you went to your party meetings, too. You worked your neighborhoods. You talked up your issues and candidates. It was a fairly constant thing, not just during the election season. Why? Because democracy is a lifestyle, not a fringe benefit of paying your taxes. Self-governance is a lot of work, but it's where you make your best friends and have your deepest satisfactions, after your family.

Just before I declared for the u.s. Senate last month, I was on a twenty-three-thousand-mile road trip to register voters. There were many housing projects and low-income neighborhoods where the people had seen nobody dropping by to talk politics since the last election. The Democrats only come around, we were told, every few years to ask for their votes, but they weren't there to listen to their problems or to help them craft political solutions. These people were of the opinion that if the Democrats won or lost, their own lives wouldn't change much. That is stripped-down politics. That is downright exploitative politics, when you come around begging for votes for your concerns, but you don't give a crouton in return. Oh yes, if your man or woman is elected, things will be better for everybody. But that is the top layer of the cake, and right now there is no cake under that frosting. We have to put it back by being involved all year long, every year, and in every neighborhood that needs political help. That is movement building—not just stumping for candidates.

You will go to your home tonight, or to your hotel room, and you will turn on all the lights and have a nice hot shower, and watch television and not even think about the electrical power that makes it all happen. If you follow the electrical wires far enough away you will find West Virginia and Kentucky communities that are being ravaged without mercy by big coal companies, protected by corrupt politicians. The coal companies cut the tops off whole mountain ranges, dump the rubble in their once-Eden-like valleys, and leave the mess to the people there. Every time it rains now, their homes flood. Giant pools of toxic sludge are everywhere, and when their dams break, toxins spill for miles. One recent spill in Inez, Kentucky, released more goo than the *Exxon Valdez*, but this is probably the first you ever heard of it.

Now, if you are worried if West Virginia and Kentucky go to the Republicans, you might first ask yourself this: Where the hell were you when they so needed your help? Where were you when residents of Cabrini-Green in Chicago, or the slums of Fort Myers or Miami or New Orleans or Los Angeles needed your organizing help and your voice added to theirs? They love their children as you love yours, and they only want decent lives. Do you think politics is just about raising money for candidates? Politics is about creatively serving the needs of your people, and the election is just the report card for how you are doing and how many people you have helped and how many people are following your leadership because you were there for them.

So don't let this new progressive alliance be another can of Betty Crocker icing for a cake that isn't there. Organize not just now to win elections, but every day to deserve to win elections.

If we can help people in distressed situations solve their problems, they will be there to speak out on the larger issues that concern many of the people in this room. But few people will speak up about global warming until they have a warm house for their own children. Building a national constituency for change requires that we first work together to solve a wide range of personal issues for people.

The new meet-ups that have become possible and popular this year are a powerful force for change, but only when they go further than being just a gathering of like-minded citizens; they must become organizing units for bringing in people who are not yet like-minded. They must become organizing units for people who will do more than sit around and share their feelings about politics; they must be platoons that go out and get real politics done.

This is an amazing moment in all of our lives, and in the life of our great nation. Never has our democracy been so challenged, and never have so many patriots of every age risen up to take their part in its defense. In the last two years, never have I been less proud of my government or more proud of its people.

■ ■ ■

While I was speaking, Dennis cornered Kucinich's campaign manager, who had a reputation for running an efficient organization. Add a little Trippi and other experts, and maybe we could patch it together. But, no, she wanted only to go home and forget about politics. She had someone on her team, however, who would be perfect for us, she said. We hired her recommended manager the next week over tea at a New Hampshire farm.

Before we left Boston, I gave a speech at historic Faneuil Hall as part of an event trying to influence the Democratic delegates. It was July 27. I mention it only because I was so moved to be there and to speak in the same place where so many had spoken before:

> Feel this place under you and around you. Know where you are. All the world knows the story of how the Americans became a free people, how they declared their independence, how they devised a constitution that is still an engine of fairness, of improvement, of justice and freedom. But the story seems remote sometimes. So feel this place under you. Know where you are. Remember who we are. This room, these walls, echoed the words of Sam Adams as he

stood in this place and reminded Americans who they were and what they must do. In this room we Americans heard George Washington and Daniel Webster shape the new Republic. In this room William Lloyd Garrison helped define an American value system that could no longer admit of human slavery, and he defined nonviolent resistance in a way that was persuasive with Ruskin in England and Tolstoy in Russia and Gandhi in South Africa and India—and from Gandhi back to Martin Luther King in America. From this room! And here spoke Susan B. Anthony to move our engine of equality forward again. And here spoke John Kennedy and so many other Americans who loved freedom and justice and who pushed us to be a better people, ever moving us along the Freedom Trail.

Feel this place. Remember who you are and why you are here and understand that all of them and all of us are of one mind and sometimes of one place. We are in this room. And perhaps those who have come before us are in this room yet, to see their work continue and be the spirits of our inspiration. Feel this neighborhood around you: The street corner of the Boston Massacre is but a few steps behind me; the Tea Party was but a few steps behind you. Revere's house, the Old North Church, are but across the way, still there, still living containers for our aspirations and our shared courage.

19

A CAMPAIGN FROM OUR TOWN

*I*n speeches at the end of daily walks, I talked about Senator Gregg and the influence of special interest money, of course, but mostly I slammed George Bush's attacks on peace, Social Security, real homeland security, and the deficit. I claimed that the advances made by the "Greatest Generation" were being destroyed. A lot of people were deciding that the ninety-four-year-old woman with the bad cough might be too old for six years in the Senate, but was dead right about George Bush.

Campaigns are stressful. There were competing visions of which way we should go. We held a meeting in my living room to iron things out. Blue thought she should move on. She didn't like the tensions and the anger. Somehow, we all understood that she was our coal-mine canary. She was carrying the soul of the future for us.

Jane, a management consultant who worked in New York City but who lived in Peterborough and helped us run our meetings and keep on schedule, had a tear in her eye. "Then that's it for the campaign," she said in a whisper. The factions came together in that moment. There would be other problems in the days ahead, but everyone understood that we were doing this for the future. Blue stayed, though she spent more and more of her time organizing college campuses. She took Rosie on the road.

During all this, my walking the state continued. Jim drove me to the far corners of the state to walk the postal roads, and our brass band and banners made a splash. We had "Burma Shave" signs posted all over the state. They were series of four or five signs along the two-lane highways, with a dozen different messages, such as: "Her Campaign Cash / Is Fat-Cat Free / She'll Represent / Just You and Me! / Doris "Granny D" Haddock for US Senate." And: "When Will Congress / Work for Me? / I'm Sending In / My Granny D!"

We had a veritable factory of volunteers turning out the handmade signs and installing them. A former Justice Department lawyer, Maury

Geiger, now from the north woods of New Hampshire—who was then and remains today a major force working for humanitarian conditions in Haiti—slept on the floor of our little campaign headquarters in Peterborough, waking each dawn to oversee another crew of sign makers and installers.

The people of Peterborough piled into the office to gather up the signs and posts and drive them to locations across the state. They brought food, hosted barbecues and even a barn dance. It was democracy to make Thornton Wilder proud.

Looming ahead had always been the live, televised candidate debate. I was petrified at the thought of it. If I didn't hear the questions well, or if I got flustered and couldn't think of what to say, it would be the end, and deeply embarrassing to all my friends. My opponent was a polished debater and was Bush's sparring partner in preparation for Bush's debate with Kerry.

The night for our debate finally came, and I did make him answer to his campaign donor conflicts and his support for disastrous Bush policies. The high moment was when he, after describing a sublime moment fishing in a stream, asked me what I could do to improve on his environmental record.

"I hope you didn't eat that fish, Senator," I answered. I attacked him for the levels of mercury in New Hampshire streams, partly a product of the Bush administration's loosening of environmental regulations on coal-fired power plants. I whacked him for warrantless wiretapping allowed by Bush's Patriot Act, which the senator erroneously denied.

I looked and sounded my age, all right, but I held my own, considering. Most of the television viewers polled gave me the debate, though they were probably being kind.

There was something of a coup in the headquarters in the final few weeks. The Kucinich folks wanted to do house parties and pull me off the road to just do speeches. Dennis and some others thought it was far too late for house party organizing, and he insisted that the walk should continue right up to Election Day. He said we needed to put all our few remaining dollars into television ads, and the staff should all take cuts by half in order to do it.

Dennis threatened to leave if it was going to be belated house parties and no walking and no TV. In fact he had given up and was packed one morning when Blue, who is taller than Dennis, stood behind him with a big knife to his neck — an angry Lady of the Lake. She suggested he stay and fight. He laughed, but he assented. When he laid out the case to me, I agreed with him.

We doubled our poll numbers in the last days of the campaign, but of course it was far from what we needed to win — not that I ever really expected to win. Good God! Six years in Washington trying to hear everybody and stay awake? I shuddered at the thought of winning. But we had to swing New Hampshire into the blue. Maybe we owed New Hampshire that.

Fred and Leslie kept the band playing behind me, and we hit the downtown sidewalks all over the state. We were in the final flow. It was more fun than anything I could ever have imagined. We were back in the joy business, and the red and gold leaves swirled around us as we sped across the state toward the last evening of the last and longest day.

When we arrived in the parking lot of our headquarters after the very last mile walked, the last interview, the last handshake, I stood for a moment looking at the beauty of the place and marveling at the adventure that had come my way so late.

If this were a novel we would have won for sure. We went from a fraction of the vote to, on election night, over a third, which was more than respectable, and was double what many of the pundits had predicted. If a ninety-four-year-old woman can get that many votes against the most popular incumbent senator in the nation, and without a dime of political action committee money, every incumbent should worry. President Bush had predicted I would get 10 percent. We actually won in the few precincts where we had the funds to advertise — Portsmouth and Keene, especially. Keene had wonderful organizing, so our victory there may have had less to do with us than with those party volunteers, but we all did everything we could to make it happen. Keene provided a fat enough margin to swing the whole state into the presidential blue.

New Hampshire became the only swing state that had swung to Bush in 2000 to swing back to blue in 2004. It was by nine thousand votes. It wasn't enough to give the nation the new leadership it needed, but, by God, we had done what we could, and it was something. As we watched New Hampshire go blue on the television on election night, the pain of the national election faded. All you can ever worry about is your own effort.

The election night party was in a big room in the Peterborough building where we had our office; it was an old mill. Just outside the great windows of our party, the river, under a three-quarter moon, flowed over the mill dam in a smooth hump of black silk. A billion red and gold leaves rode upon it.

Through the evening, more and more townspeople arrived with food and high spirits. I danced with Jim, Dennis, and every man in the place. Fred, Leslie, and the boys played a hundred songs. Blue arrived from the seacoast where she had been shuttling students and voters to the polls. More than that, she had led rallies.

When Kerry was late for a rally at the Manchester airport on the last Sunday of the campaign, Blue, whose get-out-the-vote organizing had made her a bit of a celebrity among the younger campaigners, was ushered to the stage. She spoke from her heart, describing her journey from apathy to political engagement. She told the young people that they have the power; that the politicians are only there to work for us, to represent our dreams and values. The crowd was silent for her. The hush that came over them was deeply moving to many. When she finished, they went wild, raising the roof of that great hangar. Kerry finally arrived, giving Blue a hug and making a speech that was an anticlimax.

It would take a couple of weeks to take down the campaign, return equipment, collect all the signs. It was in the beauty of late autumn.

Blue gave Dennis a little tattoo of a bluebird on the back of his left shoulder—something of a breakthrough for a very conventional chap. It was one of the Live Free or Die birds from the back of Rosie—a little bird to whisper in his ear whenever he might need some encouragement from our days on the road.

I learned things in all that time. I learned that issues aren't really as important in politics as everyone thinks. Issues have traction only in the vacuum of authentic leadership. I learned that there are enough people for the Democrats to win any election, if the party will start representing people instead of incumbent politicians, and if they will please go to where the people are waiting for them and need them. If the party ever starts looking like old Rosie instead of limousines, we can't lose. We need a year-round presence in every tough neighborhood, and, yes, we can afford that if we will let go of the downtown offices and the consultants.

Authenticity is what people long for. If the parties are to represent the people, they have to cut loose from the elites that have dominated and misused them for so long.

■ ■ ■

So that's my story. In the crush of life, my old life faded away and new lives kept cropping up. I lost contact with Lulu, Bobbie, Vera, and Ramona a very long time ago. The last I heard of each of them was that they were doing well, with only Bobbie living an artist's life. How they all came out in the end, I do not know. The Depression sent us into lives we could not have predicted.

In 1956 I was in New York City for my son-in-law's graduation from medical school. Naturally, we went to a Broadway play. It was *The Lark*, based on the story of John of Arc and starring Julie Harris. I was moved by the play. I was awestruck to see Miss Harris move so beautifully and speak so perfectly. Then, in the late '70s, I saw her in *The Belle of Amherst*, which was unforgettable. She used a shawl brilliantly to represent her different ages. Her voice is Emerson-perfect, though she went elsewhere. For the whole delicious time of that performance at the Longacre, I imagined that she was me, that I had not married Jim, that I had moved to New York with Bobbie and Vera and Ramona and maybe even Lulu, and we had struggled there and got bit parts, then had gotten into major plays and leading parts. I think I could have done it. I would not have wanted to do it, as I had come to love my husband and my children more than anything. I was not sad for my life, but I was overcome with the sadness of the fact that we cannot live all the lives we want. But Miss Harris, who maybe looked a bit like me when I was young, was doing the play brilliantly. If I could but think of her as a part of me, and me as a part of her, which is the way we must always think of each other, then I was everywhere and I did everything. And because Miss Harris may not have had the time to work on all the civic issues she might have wished, the part of her in me did all that.

I mentioned that memory once to Linda Poras, the mother of the filmmaker Marlo Poras, who had accompanied me though that wild year of the Senate campaign. I had no idea that she could and would do something about that memory of mine. In Boston one evening, I attended a theater showing of Marlo's film about our adventures. After the theater was dark, someone sat next to me and held my hand. I did not know, until after the film when Marlo introduced some people attending, that the person beside me was Julie Harris, who, it happened, was Linda's old friend. So how strange that, that one evening, I was up on the screen and Julie was in the audience, and there was not an inch between us or our lives.

When I was finally back in my quiet home and alone, I received a package. In it was a nice note from Miss Harris, and a beautiful shawl, which she said she had always loved and would like me to have. It was like the one she used in *The Belle of Amherst*. I cried into the shawl, but not in sadness. My life has been perfect in its way, though climbing back to the creative life that I knew on Joy Street took a remarkable number of years. But I did it, and so many people were so very ready to help me, as will help anyone who tries in earnest.

Blue Broxton is a successful artist in Los Angeles now, having gone back to college. She has continued her creative life at an age when I faltered. Dennis is writing books in Arizona and I suppose doing some politics. Jim is making maple syrup for his grandchildren and for other children who materialize from these woods.

And for me, I am satisfied. It has been grand. I am not tired. I would happily take another hundred years if I could.

20

LESSONS FROM MY CENTURY

*T*here were times when I feared I was walking through the last days of the American democracy. I don't think so anymore. Yes, the necessary human scale of politics is under fire from overlarge corporations and a government that has forgotten its own Bill of Rights, but the energy of people, the organizing tools available to them, and the spirit of freedom will overcome those things. The environment will be saved, too, because we really have no choice but to do so.

The main thing to remember is that the nation is the sum of what we do as individuals. If you drive a gas hog, you can't end wars, no matter whom you vote for. What we do as individuals adds up as national policy, so we have to get ourselves right.

And to fight the big fights ahead, we have to be strong and awake. If I may offer some basic advice along that line, it is this: When you wake up in the morning, do actually wake up to the new day around you. Don't fall victim to the disease of abstraction, thinking that it is simply a cookie-cutter Tuesday or Wednesday or whatever the calendar says, when it is in fact a completely new experience, only borrowing its name for convenience. We are hurtling through an unexplored universe of unimaginable size, and each moment takes us into entirely new territory of space and time.

Occasionally it all seems a little too much. I actually do sometimes have to make an effort to engage the new day. Under my covers, I waken. The comfort of a warm bed is weighed against the struggles of old age. I count to one hundred. I do it as fast or slow as I please, but when I get to one hundred, I have to get out of bed, for that is the rule. And once I show up in the new day, I'm fine. I have my tea, and then I look to see how my friends are doing and what we might do to cause some trouble.

Gardening and walks, a birdfeeder near your kitchen window, will help you connect with the day. We do ourselves a great favor each morning if we simply go out and walk and experience things for ourselves. We each come from the earth. We grow from it, eat of it, eventually go back to it, and so a good relation with it gives us our daily energy.

I walk like a curious child. In fact I think it is good to indulge your immaturity. There is a child in me who, even now, wants to see the other side of the mountain, wants to save the world from a biplane, wants to be in the company of handsome men and fascinating people. Our childhood curiosity, our sexual drive, our sense of adventure, our hunger for a heroic and meaningful life are with us always. You should use that energy. Use it in your imagination, and use it to help you get out of bed. And don't forget to go to the salon and get the works, plus a new outfit. Know how to wear a hat and a scarf to turn heads. We are simple creatures, and our energy comes from simple places.

Guide that energy with some well-considered opinions and, from them, solid values that become more solid over the years with the help of an open mind. Values that get more solid with the help of a closed mind are, of course, a great danger.

Good values are the foundation of good leadership — leadership for yourself and those around you. You must be enough in command of your own values to have an opinion about what should be done in the world, what needs doing in the house today, and who should be invited to dinner next Saturday.

I did have the great pleasure of being around people who knew just what should be done. My father, then Alan Ayer was like that, and Robert E. Peabody, then my own husband, and dear Elizabeth and Max Foster. My son is like that now.

It is amazing what a powerful people-magnet good values are. There was never a weekend at the Dundee farm of the Fosters when there were not two or three professors from Harvard or scientists, astronomers, or writers from the region. And if Robert Frost were to come to dinner, which he certainly did, he would have to recite something for his supper or join in one of our impromptu plays. Why? — because Max said so, and Max's values made him a lovely force of nature.

One afternoon putting in a vegetable garden with Max's wife, Elizabeth, I asked her where Max got this habit of inviting such people to dinner. This was, I believe, the last time we gardened together before her stroke. We were both quite old.

"It came naturally. It was just the sort of thing both our fathers did all the time, and their fathers, and so on. Didn't you meet my sister, Isabel? Her husband was a master of that sort of thing. Did she tell you that story about Adlai Stevenson?"

Yes, she did, and so I will tell it to you now, and then we will put away this book.

Elizabeth's sister Isabel had married Paul Harper, the son of William Rainey Harper, the first president of the University of Chicago. I had met Isabel back in the 1960s, when I was on a trip through the Midwest. It struck me that she, Elizabeth's sister, looked quite like me. That, I thought, might have been the reason Elizabeth took an instant liking to me, many years earlier. Brothers and sisters were much closer back in the days when there were fewer distractions like TV and autos, and more difficulty in traveling to see each other once everyone left home. So maybe my being around was a comfort to Elizabeth.

Isabel had recently lost her husband, so Elizabeth asked me to drop in on her, since I would be near.

Isabel laughed when she told me the Adlai story.

"Paul heard a young lawyer named Adlai Stevenson speak downtown and thought he was very good and should run for something. Of course, Adlai's father was big in politics here, and his grandfather, Adlai the First, ran for vice president under Bryan, so he certainly had the genes for it. Paul asked me to put together one of our evenings where all the leading lights come have dinner and meet some young rising star. I sent out the dinner invitations and got a note that the Stevensons would be delighted to attend."

Isabel showed me the unusual stairway up from the entry to the parlor and said that the stairs had saved the evening.

"Well, all Paul's big friends were up there and finally the Stevensons arrived a bit late. I had invited the wrong A. Stevenson. The man was a high school janitor, and he came with his wife. Paul and I met them at the door and, without spilling the beans, determined who they were and what Mr. Stevenson did for a living. Paul asked me to help them with their coats while he went back up to the affair.

"By the time the Stevensons got up the stairs, Paul had clued in everyone. Paul tapped his cocktail glass and announced, 'And please welcome the Stevensons. Mr. Stevenson, as you know, is the gentleman we are honoring tonight for his work in keeping our high school so beautiful for the children of our community.'"

In fact, through the evening, Mr. Stevenson, when asked, shared many ideas for improving the schools that were received as great advice by those attending, many of whom had the power to make changes.

Years later, Isabel bumped into Mrs. Stevenson at a horse event. It happened that they both had grown up with horses. Isabel, like her sister Elizabeth, kept horses all her life, and so she invited Mrs. Stevenson to come ride with her. They became good friends. When Mr. Stevenson died, Isabel built a guesthouse so Mrs. Stevenson could live with them. It had its own horse stall so that Mrs. Stevenson could open a window in the morning and give her horse some sugar or an apple. She lived there until she passed away, providing Isabel with her best friend in later life.

I asked Isabel if Mrs. Stevenson ever knew about the invitation being a mistake.

"She knew immediately, somehow. But she never let on with her husband. She said the evening was one of the highest points of his life."

I was very moved—the story still moves me—to think how Paul's kindness and quick thinking had resulted in so much good. The ability to turn disappointments into opportunities often results in the best features of our lives. Life is tough, and it is supposed to be, or we shouldn't learn a thing, and our souls might not grow an inch deeper or wider, as they must, but there is no reason we can't turn those troubles into love and beauty.

When Elizabeth died, I took her gardening hat and walked across the United States with it. The long walk was a time to turn all my losses into love, and a time to step out of all the shadows I had found for myself.

I had a long history of inhabiting shadows. In my midlife, I cared for my forever-dying mother-in-law. She was a remarkable woman in many ways, but for eight of my precious young years, she was relentlessly needy and I became her servant. But then she died.

My husband loved me completely, but his image of me became my outer limits. I became his servant, especially in the ten years of his Alzheimer's disease. But then he died. And so did my best friend, Elizabeth, who was so much my social mentor that I was constrained by her opinion of me. Her father, by the way, was the head of the Rockefeller Foundation, and her grandfather founded the Chautauqua movement, and she was an author herself and full of wisdom and encouragement for me, though I was of course in her shadow. But then she died.

All the loving stones that were leaned upon me came off. All the old embers under me were deep in ash but ready still. If my creative life had been interrupted by the imperatives of living, it stretched before me now on an open road, though I was nearly ninety. I would have to do a lot of living before I reached one hundred, I decided.

Old Pete Seeger had written me a nice letter when my book came out about the walk. He said the book, like *Silent Spring* and *Walden*, had changed his life. I didn't really believe that, and wouldn't want his life changed anyway, but it was so kind that I wanted to say thank you in person. We met a few times and have corresponded. He keeps going, and that has helped me keep going. He has a song, you know, called "Quite Early Morning," that will keep you walking and singing and tuned to the fact that we are all walking in beauty, and others will take up for us, and for love, when we have faded happily away. You should listen.

LAST DELIVERED SPEECH

Doris Haddock was honored on the occasion of her one hundredth birthday in the chambers of New Hampshire's governor. Several hundred people attended. In her thank-you remarks, Doris said:

That you would all take time from your busy life to be here is a great gift to me, and I thank you for it.

People have been asking me how I feel about the recent decision by the Supreme Court to strike down some of the campaign finance reforms that I walked for and have been working on for a dozen or so years.

When I was a young woman, my husband and I were having dinner at the Dundee home of a friend, Max Foster, when a young couple rushed through the door breathless to say that they had accidentally burned down the guest cabin down by the river. Max stood up from his meal. He set his napkin down. He smiled at the young couple and he said,

"That's wonderful. We have wanted to build something special down there on the river, and this will give us a chance to do that without feeling guilty about getting rid of that old cabin."

Well, I guess the Supreme Court has burned down our little cabin, but, truth be told, it was pretty drafty anyway. We had not really solved the problem of too much money in politics, and now we have an opportunity to start clean and build a system of reforms that really will do the trick. . . .

Thank you again, very much indeed, for absolutely everything.

LAST UNDELIVERED SPEECH

Written and meant for delivery at the 2010 Fighting
Bob La Follette Fest in Wisconsin, an annual gathering
of national reformers

Thank you very much.

Nations, history has shown us, have a state of mental health. A nation may be open and positive, hardworking, and fully confident of its future. It may send great white fleets around the world and humans into space. A nation may also be angry, self-destructive, cruel. We are individuals, and we are parts of a whole. The whole can be as troubled or as ecstatic and positive as an individual. You all know this very well, and you know that, at the present time, America is angry and divided and rather like a mentally disturbed person. Many of its citizens are turning away from obvious truths and embracing angry and dangerous fantasies.

If someone you know flies off the handle in an uncharacteristic way and will not listen to the clear facts, perhaps his dear wife will take you aside and explain that there is a major problem in the family to account for the outburst. It's hard to settle arguments and put away anger when we are desperately anxious about our future and our family.

That sort of anxiety is driving America's politics today. Where does it come from? Anger and blindness to the facts are the twin children of powerlessness—powerlessness over one's own and one's family's future.

That anxiety is manipulated by masters of self-interest. In the 1950s, as great corporations began to wash away the family businesses of Main Street, the anger of those middle-class families should have been directed against those corporations and the political officials in league with them. Instead, anger was purposely and methodically redirected against a phantom Communist threat inside America, against the civil rights of blacks, and against any expansion of government into worker protection and consumer protection. Because the anxiety was misdirected, it was not brought to bear on the proper cause of the anxiety, and so the anxiety only grew.

Corporations and the very wealthiest people began to finance the election campaigns of their foot soldiers in Congress. They financed talk radio and propaganda television. We now see millions of people whose anxiety has been hijacked and redirected against their own best interests.

In the Reagan years, all the stops were taken off things like hostile corporate takeovers and the rise of new monopolies, so that even the most ethical companies were forced to ship their jobs overseas and shutter their plants in American towns and cities to avoid hostile take-overs. This was all very profitable for the wealthiest elite. You might wonder why these people have allowed things to go so far that the earth of their grandchildren is now endangered—perhaps fatally—and the answer is that they do not care about their children or grand-children, so long as they themselves have the longest yachts in Monaco harbor.

From those yachts are sent instructions that control what Fox News watchers and talk radio listeners will be upset about tomorrow. This undead army will be used to stop all real progress toward real solu-tions, and the mass anxiety of the people will grow even greater, even as their homes are taken from them and their foods are poisoned. All this engineering needs ready enemies, and so it is the Mexican immi-grants or Arabs anywhere are the Other who now have the honor of being scapegoats and diversions. We could, after all, stop illegal im-migration by improving economic conditions in Latin America, and we could end Arab anger by moving our economy from oil to solar, but those are big-business considerations for proper discussion in the yachts off Monaco, not in our pretend Congress. The yachts off Monaco are sending no sons and daughters to the oil wars.

So the anger of anxiety grows. Guns and ammunition now flow into our communities in semi trucks. The politics polarizes to the extent that some have no moral or patriotic objection to sabotaging the econ-omy if it will mean more votes in the next election. And facts as plain as day—as plain as a birth certificate—will be insulted and burned in the streets.

If I were the president of the United States looking at all this, what would I do?

I would do a great deal.

I would use administrative powers to do as much as I could to return a sense of personal power to people. Every notch will help defuse anger. I would require federally insured banks to have human beings answer the bank's phones, and have local human beings assigned to personally help every customer, with full authority to make most decisions regarding those accounts. I would find out in which other industries federal leverage might permit similar returns to the human scale, so that people had more daily moments when they did not feel so powerless against the machinery of modern life. Just because we have the technological power to dehumanize our world, doesn't mean we should do so. I would find a way to dismantle the telephone answering robots and put a million young people to work overnight. It is a kind of torture, after all. If my call is indeed important to them, let them hire a human being to help me.

As the president, I would look at the companies that sell things to the federal government. I would give a purchasing preference to those companies that dumped their computerized, outsourced telephone systems and other systems of human contact in favor of a more human-scaled operation.

I would give a thousand preferences to small businesses. I would order the agencies of government to buy American products when possible, even at a premium. Without turning my back on the environment or on worker rights and safety, I would start a campaign against the kinds of red tape that inhibit the creation of Main Street businesses and small-scale manufacturers. The object of these moves is simple: to give more people a sense of control over their own lives and futures.

This is not some libertarian rant. The far right would have us living in some everyone-for-themselves nightmare world. Government at its best is just the lot of us making some decisions together for the benefit of all. Getting back to that, and getting away from the "them versus us" notion of government is crucial. Getting rid of the bloat of bureaucracy is an essential part of it. We can move with the right wing on this issue—though we may get off the bus a few stops before they do. I expect a roomful of citizens could come up with a thousand things that make them feel disempowered and that might be changed. Little empowerments can build toward more meaningful power. People ultimately need to believe, and correctly so, that their daily efforts will bear the harvest they have earned.

They need to own their own financial records just as they own their own medical records, and they should therefore have the right to opt out of credit reporting systems. People's names and addresses and e-mail addresses should never be sold without their permission. All the fine print in contracts—things you must click on and agree to if you are to get access even to things you have purchased, should be outlawed for purchases of under, say, a thousand dollars. You shouldn't have to sign a ten-page contract to buy a damn song or to use the program that plays it. All those little things are insulting to us, and they add up. Maybe we will need to take our shoes off at the airport for a while yet, but we shouldn't have to bow so low to every company that tells us to.

Stores ought to look for shoplifters and stop them, but devices that scan and beep at the doorways, and clerks who stop you at the door before leaving to examine your basket and your receipt are making an accusation that you are probably a thief, and Americans should not be accusing each other of such things without probable cause. It is dehumanizing. Our dignity demands a presumption of innocence not only in the courts, but also in our daily lives. These little things that eat away at our dignity ultimately make us angry and alienated. So end those practices. Put consumer and government pressure to bear against companies that will not abide by a new golden rule of personal treatment in America. When people are treated with an expectation of honor, they tend to respond. The few that do not are not worth worrying about.

Further, when we have a Congress that again represents the people, we need to return to the states the authority to limit interest rates that can be charged on loans and credit cards. States used to have that power, and rates were generally limited to not much over 10 percent, but the interstate banking lobby purchased Congress, and we are all now paying for their yachts as a result. This can be a states' rights issue, and we can do business with the right wing on this, if they can break the hypnosis imposed on them by big business.

The United States of America has an interest in the development of small, family-run local and regional businesses. Those businesses are good for the economy, good for communities, good for families, good for personal empowerment, and good for democracy. When we have us a Congress again, let's create a corporate tax system that discourages businesses from growing larger than they need to be. A computer company and an automobile company may need to be large, but there is no reason for general merchandise stores to be overlarge. There is no reason for insurance companies or media companies to be overlarge. Returning the economy to a more local and more human scale is important and necessary for our political, cultural, and ecological health.

While we are at it, we should get rid of corporate-run prisons. What is a greater insult to an American than to be locked up by a corporation? Anyone in that circumstance ought to have a right to resist. It is a science-fiction-like horror that insults all of us.

If we fail to act on these matters, the sense of personal disempowerment will grow, and also its anger and its violence.

Returning a more human scale to our economy would also create quite a few jobs and quite a few new businesses. If a U.S. president would take up an aggressive campaign to return human scale and its personal power to Americans, I don't think he or she would find too many opponents, except in the yachts off Monaco. They would of course instruct Fox News to rail against this return to the stone age. But the anger that fuels their toxic enterprise and others like it would dissipate, and we might soon have a governable country again.

The idea of a social safety net, while constantly attacked by the wealthy elite and the Fox undead, provides important ways to reduce the kinds of anxiety that otherwise disrupt society and democracy. If parents know their children will be able to attend college, that they themselves will have a secure old age, and that the only time people will sleep outdoors in America is when they are camping, they will be better neighbors, better parents, better spouses, better and more productive workers, and better Americans.

If there is one thing that would guarantee any president's election or re-election, it is this final suggestion: a president could administratively modify the procurement code of the federal government so that companies that do more than a million dollars worth of business with the federal government annually must not lobby the federal government in any way except in open hearings. This disempowerment would result in a grand re-empowerment of average citizens, who then would stand a chance being heard by their elected representatives. With every notch—and that would be a big one—anger subsides, racism subsides, we step away from the precipice now before us, and we move toward a much better America.

These are ideas someone might package and promote. A joining of left and right might be possible regarding this package. A president in search of a little triangulation might even listen.

Frankly, I don't think we have much time to waste. Anger is what is in our way, and it comes from the disempowerment of us all.

Thank you very much.

CLOSING NOTE TO THE READER

I first met Doris when she was nearly ninety and walking across the United States for campaign finance reform in 1999–2000. It was my pleasure to work with her on her political efforts during her walk and in the years following. For the last several Februaries of her life she came to my home in the West to work on this, her second and final memoir.

She died in March of 2010, a month after her one hundredth birthday and two weeks after finishing the interviews that became this book. Her funeral was held in the Dublin Community Church, attended by her townspeople, by political leaders and artists, and by friends from far lands.

She was walking three and four miles a day in the last week of her life. She was feeling very fit until about three days before the onset of a sudden respiratory illness that took her life.

All the time I knew her, she was young and fearless, much like her son, Jim, who passed away in March of 2011, and who filled the old church as his mother had done.

It should be said that, for New Hampshire, they were not that unusual.

DENNIS MICHAEL BURKE